The Force Behind Espionage Into Corruption

One cannot help feeling shameful of blaming the Western World for African social problems. Still, an African like myself will always look into the history of relationships between the Africans and Europeans before casting any blame.

The history of mankind documents that man originated in Africa. British history asserts that history of human civilization starts with the Egyptians. US historians politely contradict the British history, stating that history of civilization starts in the Middle East–Mesopotamia–the land between two rivers. Still, Egyptians believe that when they die, their spirits go to Africa south of the Sahara, West Africa, to be precise.

The difference between gods and men is men believe gods are better than they are–hence, they worship them.

What I am saying here is the gods are better than men, or since men worship the gods, the gods should be more civilized than men. Since the gods model the behavior of men, Egyptians–being men–were civilized by the gods. Well, this is a "far out" speculation, but it actually demonstrates that historians, American or British, knew nothing about the history of Africa besides Egypt and Ethiopia.

How about the Meroe and Kush Empires before the Egyptians? *King Solomon's Mine* by Ridder Hargard is fiction, yet it reveals a lot of what was Africa before Egypt.

I must admit it is hard to attach dates on what was Africa before Egypt, but that does not mean Africans were not there before the acclaimed European and US history. The modern time reveals a lot of what was Africa in comparison to what was Europe.

A.D. 1069 reveals much of what was Africa via the Songhai Empire and what was Europe via England at A.D. 1060 when the Duke of Normandy invaded England. Of course all these seem like fairy tales when an African looks at himself and thinks he is a sorry sight and chooses to perceive himself and his society through the European perception. Or he seems to prostitute himself to the European and his societies as an economic commodity and a social misfit so as to be able to present himself as a human being or Africa as a community of human beings in the world.

It is obvious—very obvious—that Wole Soyinka is a scholar. But before I get carried away, let me say this: Mr. Soyinka is not different from the African Academia elite. It just happens that his present role in Nigerian political crises reveals his "ignorance," his "diplomacy" game, or his refusing to "look at history in the face" with his perception or slogan on the word "democracy." It does not matter which democracy he is advocating for Nigerians or Africans—Athenian-Greek, Roman, British, Hitler German, French, or US democracy.

I have seen this fellow Nigerian's photograph and can imagine he is or may be of the same age as I. This means we must, in one way or another, have used the same textbooks in social studies on African or Nigerian history.

It bothers me how my perception of politics in Africa and African society is different from Mr. Wole Soyinka's. It is obvious that European governments, by the time they came to Nigeria, were a generation of Greek democracy via Roman democracy. This means the Europeans were using their democracy when the Pope divided the world into two, giving the west to Spain and the east to Portugal (Papal Bull of Demarcation).

It was that same democracy the Europeans visited Africa with and used to enslave Africans to the extent that Nigeria, our country (Wole Soyinka's and mine), was known on African maps as Slave Coast, as Ghana was known as Gold Coast and Cote De Voire as Ivory Coast.

When the Europeans found slavery less profitable, it was the same democracy they used to colonize Africa; and after African countries become independent, they borrowed or were imposed upon with the same democracy that Mr. Wole Soyinka and his gang of academic elite are forcing on Nigeria, which hundreds of Nigerians died for and which has so reduced their human dignity they are ashamed of their very beings.

Anybody who knows that democracy directed American minds to drop the atomic bomb at Hiroshima; napalm bombs on Koreans, Vietnamese, Cambodians, Iraqis, and recently, Kosovo, knows that nobody in his right mind should cohort with the advocates of such callous social philosophy.

It is the same democracy that the South African peacemaker President Mandela, with the Ghanaians and the US, used to assassinate General Abacha. It is the same democracy they used to manipulate Nigerian politics which appointed Nigerian Head of State General Abubarkar and elected General Obasanjo Nigerian president in a swindled election.

Look at Congo, Algeria, South Africa, Rwanda, Kenya, Somalia, Ethiopia, Sierra Leone, and Liberia. The civil wars are defending democracy, and citizens of these countries have been dying for this European democracy for more than one hundred years.

Africans have suffered so much in this democracy that every African should learn to not only fear the word but to wipe it from their memories. The word has so dehumanized Africans that some hate their Negroid qualities without examining them.

It is not our Negroid qualities which are inferior; it is the European and US abuse of Africa and Africans with their democracy which dehumanizes Africans.

I heard education would have taught Africans that democracy is whatever Europeans and Americans are using to exploit Africans and Africa to death. One does not have to study the economic geography of Africa to know the gods have blessed us with natural resources. Now think of the millions of Africans who were enslaved from the continent, and some of their generation look at Africa today and exclaim "Well, I'd like to visit there, but I sure do not wish to live there." Imagine Nigeria at present producing millions of barrels of oil every day and having to import the same oil from the Europeans who export that oil from Nigeria. Look at Congo living in poverty and at Mobutu, who assassinated Lumumba with the help of the Western World—with the promise to do exactly what Lumumba planned to do for the Congolese. Well, Mobutu allowed Belgium, Britain, and the US to come back to Congo, ruled Congo with the same European democracy for more than thirty years, and increased his family savings up to five billion dollars.

Somalia has no natural resources as Congo does, but it has a good geographical location. The US developed Somalian ethnic squabbles into a full-blown national civil war in the name of democracy, mainly to sell their arms to the Somalians and control the location.

The US got involved in Nigeria as far back as the late forties through Chief Obafemi Awolowo, purposely to swindle the Nigerian presidency with their democracy. Nigeria has everything the US needs to control and "own" Africa and Africans. For every four Africans, one is a Nigerian. Nigeria, like Congo, is a very wealthy country. Also, Nigerian oil is the best in the world.

Chief Awolowo could not deliver Nigeria to the US, which then silently switched their attention to Chief Abiola with a US company contract of billions in of dollars. Abiola, like Chief Awolowo, could not deliver. General Babangida stopped him cold at the Nigerian polls.

Chief Abiola was encouraged to declare himself president of Nigeria. Nigerian police arrested him. The man died in prison defending US democracy in Nigerian politics!

The US recruited the self-appointed South African peacemaker and US democracy peddler, President Mandela, and Ghana to assassinate General

Abacha. General Abacha died within a week after catching them in the plot to assassinate him. They managed to stifle General Abacha's investigation. The same gang went ahead and bought the Nigerian military, who helped them to install US democracy in Nigeria via General Obasanjo.

That democracy has been alive and well in Nigeria for the last twelve months and has failed to produce wonders in both Nigerian society and economics. The same democracy has everything it needs to turn South Africa into a heaven on earth, with their errand boy President Mandela as their captain of the ship. President Mandela ran the full course of his presidency with all the support he needed from the Western World and the US. Well, President Mandela made progress in South African economics with his US democracy. He left the office, leaving South Africa as he met her–in poverty and chaos.

I have been talking about democracy in politics. How about industries?

It is sad watching African university graduates with two, three, even four degrees from the United States or European universities criticizing African governments, themselves, and their societies as armchair philosophers while their mates in Europe and the US are putting their academic philosophies into meaningful production either as a consultants or civil servants.

Nigerian President Obasanjo warned Nigerian engineers they will soon be competing with foreign engineers for contracts in Nigeria. I wanted to applaud him for such a decision, because Nigerian scholars are nothing but armchair philosophers–but I stopped myself, wishing that Africans were given the same advantages in Europe and the US Africans are treated as third class or even fourth class citizens in both Europe and the US. Some Africans have to willingly abuse their human dignity to have themselves under-employed. Some change their names, others change their hairdos, while others still have to smile at silly jokes which are abusive to either their personal dignity or to their race as Negroids. Still Europeans and Americans are treated as first class citizens in African universities, industries, and even hotels.

At the same time I am sad feeling this way against Europeans and Americans living in Africa or even visiting the continent. Africa is big and rich with an enviably healthy climate. The continent can tolerate, maintain, and accommodate the world population if the wealth and space are well managed. But this feeling of sadness plagues my brain as I watch Europe using Africa and Africans as their footmat, at the same time using African wealth to cushion their national wealth, which leaves them living in such economic opulence one cannot help envying that.

It brings sad memories to remember Patrice Lumumba and how and why he was assassinated. The knowledge that Nigeria's Jaja of Opobo was "deported" from his country to Jamaica in the Caribbean for refusing Europeans trade in his own country does not help at all.

Kwame Nkruma was also run out of his country, Ghana, because the US told him not to cohort with the USSR. His "sin" and "crime" was saying no to the Americans. It brings tears to one's eyes when such sad memories bring Africans like Ben Bella of Algeria and Modibokeita of Mali to mind. These African nationalists were lost in the US shuffle of those who they want to rule Africa.

Muammar Kaddafi of Libya is living on a borrowed time and continuously watching his back because he does not want the US and European countries dictating to him how to run is country.

Recently the US used Ghana and South Africa to assassinate General Abacha, which some Nigerians rejoice. Abacha's sin was he refused to allow the US to hand pick Nigeria's president.

I wept for Africa, not for General Abacha, at the assassination of this man. It is one thing that angry and frustrated Nigerians band themselves together and hacked their heads of states as they did to Murtala Muhammed, Alahaji Abubarkar, Tafawa, Balewa, etc. It is painful to even suspect that the US, South Africa, and Ghana planned and assassinated General Abacha in the name of US political philosophy and democracy, with a Nigerian self-appointed praise singer for the Western democracy, Wole Soyinka.

I do not know this man and do not look forward to meeting him. This man is a celebrated European novelist. They even awarded him a Nobel Prize. But in this man's ambition to identify himself as African "Acada" with European brain, he forgot that he lives in African society. It is a matter of fact that "political democracy" is mainly elections. Democracy in the society describes democracy on projection or identification of individuals. This is not a big deal for the Athenians, Romans, and the British.

However, it is the core of the US democracy—the individual rights within the society. US democracy tells its citizens they have freedom to be. That is freedom to do as they want and be what or whoever they want to be.

Americans have taken this brand of their democracy literally and have developed different kinds of individual rights, such as women's rights, homosexual rights, children's rights, and human rights, etc.

This bothers me a lot, because this is the source of corruption in Africa. The Europeans invaded Africa with their democracy; a thief is a thief when he is caught stealing. The conventional African has developed reasons for such a vivid crime and not only redefines the crime, but reclassifies the crime to a degree that it may not be perceived as a crime, but a human urge which is either inherited, learned, or caused by society.

Homosexuals in the US are now convincing that society such human action is biological. It is of course as biological as any other human action that human culture controls.

The fact is US democracy is in their written culture. The US Constitution guarantees US citizens the right to become homosexual. They try to limit the right themselves, asserting that it should be by consenting adults in privacy. The Constitution does not say it should be between consenting adults or children and adults. In fact the Constitution guarantees the individual, not a group or more of consenting adults. Remember, the pursuit of happiness in the US Constitution is for the individual and not for the group or society. Man, by nature, is a gregarious animal. Sure, he is an individual entity, but his existence depends on his gregarious nature; he (man) created his clan, village, town, city, province, or country.

Of course bureaucracy disturbs me because it is rotten in Africa because of its Western heritage based on this Western political philosophy called democracy. I am a victim of this sad heritage, and it bothers me to watch Africa and Africans destroying themselves and using African resources to build and cushion Europe and the US in their luxury. Call it obsession. Yes, I am obsessed. Call it paranoia. Yes, I am paranoid. What I know is that curiosity did not force me to write this book. It is painful to see Europe as I saw it when I was traveling around the world and know that African slaves and natural resources provided the foundation wealth which built their industries. And even at present African raw materials are maintaining their industries, while Africans and their countries are still groping blindly in disease and poverty.

I have been living in the United States for the past thirty-four years. I have been around the States and have been living in California. It hurts to know that African-Americans labored to build the US for more than four hundred years under free labor and watched the Americans treat them as people without a country–even under the nose of the US democracy.

I have reasons to be paranoid and obsessed in this book. It is not pleasant listening to Americans and Europeans condemning Africans for not being able to industrialize their countries. These critics always forget that industrialization demands capital and leisure. Africa provided them both to Europe and the US through slavery and colonialism. And after the wind of freedom blew in Africa in the early sixties, capital and leisure eluded African nations.

Since the 1960s independent African nations have been in civil wars incited by European nations and encouraged or financed by the US as they (the Western World) continue to harvest African natural resources.

The civil wars deny African nations economic development. I traced this lack of leisure in my letter to one of the Nigerian heads of state, General Abubarkari, hoping to make the general understand the difficult position in which the Western World has cornered Nigeria.

African nations have natural resources. That is obvious, but African nations need capital to be able to exploit the natural resources. How about the foreign aid from European countries and the US? The aid turned out to be another way to exploit African countries and did not take time to show their intentions.

Africa still attracts European nations and the United States like moths to a lighted window. The echoes of their rushing feet leave a sense of doom which is hovering over the continent. It appears I am lonely in this sad perception. The sadness breeds a kind of anger more like a rage in me. One can hear the echoes of their footprints still sounding in the Congo, Nigeria, Somalia, Sudan, Ethiopia, Zimbabwe, South Africa, Rwanda, Sierra Leone, and Liberia.

I am not a violent man. If one has the patience to read through this book he will equally agree that I am not a diplomat. The only thing left for me is letting the world know the source of my frustration. I am a red-blooded Negroid African, and I am fully aware of my worth on this globe. It hurts that the world has to see and understand who I am and my quality as a Negroid African not only through European perception but sadly through US description.

I hate myself for writing or speaking the English language because it is the only medium of instruction I know. The language limits my ability to tell for posterity what Europe and the US have done and are still doing to Africa and Africans.

Look around Africa from South Africa to Libya, Nigeria to Ethiopia; corruption in African countries is growing by leaps and bounds. The only direction the African social elite are leading their fellow countrymen is toward death, still toward more corruption–what a terror!

It is not my intention to frighten Africans with this book. Still, espionage into corruption is a hard fact Africans must face and eliminate or else perish.

Some Africans have taken shelter in countries outside the continent, giving the impression that Africans in the continent are responsible for the corruption in their countries and that drove them out of Africa. This is not true at all. Most of these Africans outside the continent, especially the well-to-do Africans in Europe and the US, duped their countries through their corruption dragnets, which are usually politics and civil services and Christianity in their respective countries, and made away with the loot to their adopted countries outside Africa.

The academic elite with their meal tickets, which they refer to as diplomas or degrees, talk themselves into the espionage into the corruption by pretending to criticize social and economic activities in their countries; then, once they are recognized and given offices as either politicians or civil servants, they get their hands on the keys to their countries' treasuries, which allows them to negotiate and write contracts.

It is easy to identify these agents of espionage into corruption. They are these rich Africans that self-exiled themselves or their children. They spend their riches prodigally because they did not earn the wealth out of their sweat.

Millions left behind in Africa are trapped and compelled not to escape the stifling of being trapped by the Atlantic and Indian oceans and inescapable human sufferings. These Africans are unable to get their hands on the treasuries of their respective countries. They are therefore not agents of espionage into corruption in their respective country. They are also not even recruitable into their countries' society of sin and crime. Still they are very important to the agents of espionage into corruption. These Africans are the masses—the downtrodden in the African mud.

One can safely blame the African academic elite, simply because every agent of espionage into corruption passes his educational screens, from elementary school to doctorate degree level, whether in Dar-re-Salaam, Lagos, Nsuka, Tripoli, Kampala, or Adisababa. I often wonder what Africans see in the Western educational system. Read John Mmunonye's *Oil Man of Obange*. You will agree with me that Western education is not worth the sacrifices Africans have been donating at the European education altars.

It is easy for the reader of the above paragraph to conclude I am against education. On the contrary, but any educational system that educates the child to look down on himself and his environment must not only be condemned but must be banned in African countries.

There is really a world of discoveries and goals to reach out there through education. It is easy to envy Europeans and Americans "living it up" in their societies, having choices of what to eat, when to eat, and how to prepare their food—either with a stove, microwave, oven, blender, etc. Preparing or growing their foods is no more a choice to them.

Traveling from one spot to another in both Europe and America is not only merchandized, it is now carried on with varieties of pleasures of one's choice.

Europeans and Americans attain these levels of enjoyment in their society with their educational systems. Since these Europeans and Americans invade Africans with the self-imposed ambition to "civilize the savage"— meaning the African—the African consciously donates his wealth and sacrifices his culture and leisure in his pursuit of European and American dreams through European and American education. He reasons that, "It worked for them, it must work for us"; only to find himself and his community being castrated and reduced to a mere economic consumer for European and American industries.

It is sad, terribly sad, to have the knowledge that the European countries and the US have been using Africa and Africans to create, develop, and maintain their industries without giving Africans any reward for both their labor and supply of the materials, and now they use Africans as consumers of their industrial goods as well. The feeling worsens with the knowledge the African academic and political elite are European and US drafted errand boys.

African countries' educational systems and certifications are models of European and American education systems. These certifications are the academic meal tickets among Africans. One is then left to question if Africans have any educational system of their own. It is very obvious the European and US educational systems were created and developed for the survival and comfort of both the Europeans and the US, and Africans are nothing but one of the tools to maintain this survival. Africans are therefore "designed" to remain as Europe and America's survival tools.

This also goes sadly into African politics, which is now the political marketing design in Africa. The word *democracy* must be among words there for the political parties and must be used to lace all the sentences in political speeches. If this word *democracy* is glaringly absent in any political ambition among Africans, it is very certain the snake which bit Modibo Keita, Kwame Nkruma, Patrice Lumumba, General Soni Abacha, Ben Bela, and Idi Amin is bound to scotch such African politicians.

And this is not lip service. Who in his right mind would ever think an African president would participate in a plot to assassinate another African head of state? General Abacha caught South Africa, Ghana, and the US plotting to assassinate him in Ghana a week before he was assassinated. Ghana, of course, denied having a hand in the plot. South Africa and the US treated the accusation with contempt.

South Africa went ahead to assist the US in hand picking Nigerian president General Obasanjo. The investigation on the plot to assassinate Abacha was swept under the mat.

Within this period Nigeria voluntarily went ahead to flush out suspected US "terrorists" hiding in Republic of Chad as US "good boys." Only months later, two US embassies in East Africa (Kenya and Tanzania) were blown up. Many Africans died; many more maimed.

Africans have been used as free labor by the US and also have been building and defending US property for about three centuries or more till the 1990s, and yet Africans are regarded as less than dogs in the US.

Something devastating, something really ugly has been going on between European nations and the US throughout these centuries, since the Europeans came in contact with Africans, and Africans always get the worst deal. Imagine the South African president hawking African countries for the US bidding, and in the "deal" participating in the plot which assassinated the African president. There is no explanation for such insanity. General Abacha's assassination is not different from the deaths of the Africans who died at the embassy bombing or Lumumba's death and those who died under the hands of General Mobutu or those who die in Somalia, Sierra Leone, and Liberia. These Africans who died in defense of US and European property and political philosophy and democracy are cherished memories to this author and other Africans who choose not to look the other way on how Europeans and the US abuse Africa and Africans.

The annoying thing here is that Africans blame themselves for their misfortunes. Even this book leaves the impression that Africans are corrupt. Well, winds of freedom (independence) have blown the Europeans out from Africa, politically speaking. But the European countries and the US have appointed Africans as their economic agents and remain as the African "godfathers" but stay in Europe and the US while the African politicians and academic elite remain in Africa as their errand boys.

Espionage and *corruption* should be the last words to be associated with Africans. Africans live their lives according to the dictations of their gods, and these dictations are based on strict moral code of "*Egbe beli ugo ebili, nke si ibe ya ebena nku kwapua.*" The meaning of this adage will be lost in translation, but in a nutshell it means "live and let live."

Africans lived under this moral code for centuries before the Europeans invaded them with the strange and corruptive moral code of their social philosophy on the survival of the fittest.

This European moral code was strange, very odd to Africans. Things, strange things, began happening among Africans. Chinua Achobe captured these things in his urban novel, *Things Fall Apart.* So did John Mmunonye in his *Oil Man of Obange.* The strange thing: culture became terrible. Chinua Achobe followed it up with his *No Longer at Ease* and *Man of People.*

As colonialism began turning into independence, African culture became terrible with espionage into corruption. The hope was political freedom–that European political gimmick they call "independence." It was unreal. It is like a game played on Africans to undermine their intelligence.

The independence later became a death trap for Africans. It pitched Africans against themselves in civil wars, with European nations and the US supplying the African war materials–guns, bombs, and war planes to destroy themselves–while European and American industries boomed. Still Africans could not learn. Even as they watch Congo, Nigeria, Zimbabwe, Angola, South Africa, Rwanda, Kenya, Somalia, Liberia, and Sierra Leone on fire.

Then it became terrible. Recent Nigerian political crisis removed the scales and revealed South Africa, Ghana, and the US in their plot which assassinated an African head of state, General Abacha. It revealed the African academic elite marketing European and US political philosophy in democracy in Africa, without examining the word or looking into its history in Europe, the US, or Africa.

Now Africa becomes castrated, impotent, unable to fend for her children. The blind revolting horror is now very real to Africans, who are now condemning everything African, including their very beings.

Still, condemning everything that is African is not helping either. Africans are still living in poverty, disease, and ignorance with blind faith in the Western and US political philosophy they call democracy and sacrificing their raw materials at the altars of Western and US industries which glorify them (the Africans) as their consumers. Consumers are being fed with awful and decayed US and European industrial goods–the emissaries of the living dead. I think I am becoming emotional at this blind faith Africans are giving to the European and US social philosophies, and I am continually being convinced I have every right to be. A fellow Biafran accused me of taking the war very seriously, explaining to me that both Nigerians and Biafrans were pretending to be at war during the day and at night were partying together. According to this captain in the Biafran army, they played this game of deception for almost one year.

I imagined the cost of such deceit to those Africans who call themselves Nigerians and Biafrans. One of them saw me coming back from work and was looking at me as if I was a "piece of shit" because I was not dressed as a white collar employee. My appearance convinced him I was his god's lost sheep. He would call me and keep me on the phone for hours, praying and talking Bible things to me. I tolerated him for some weeks, politely nudging him to recognize that he was not only wasting both my time and his, he was abusing African human dignity trying to catch the wind with Christianity in Los Angeles while his people are decaying in poverty, disease, and ignorance. I wondered aloud one time during his Jesus peddling why this man should consider himself blessed, singing "hallelujah" in a foreign land while eagerly watching his people waste into nothingness.

Another Nigerian was childishly comparing his town with tin sheet roofs and my small village, Atuma, and ended up laughing in my face, stating that the inferiority of my small village to towns like his in Nigeria is the source of my frustration. According to this African, Nigeria is doing fine. It is individuals like me who refuse to admit the superior human quality of the "white man" to Africans (meaning "the Negroid"). All this time he was waving his cell phone at my face, telling me occasionally that it was the symbol of his "white man's" intellectual accomplishments over the Negroid.

This African holds a degree in engineering from one of California's public universities. I treated his perception of what is wrong in African and among Africans with silence. But I was worried at this same time at the knowledge staring at my face. This man may end up one day to be my head of state. At present President Obasonjo is now ruling Nigeria for the second time. He, too, was an engineer. I wonder how this man sees his intellectual quality in comparison to that of President Carter, Clinton, or Prime Minister Blair!

Africa has made Europe and the US what they are economically, and this African engineer is blind to this fact. I thought of the school curriculums which brought him up academically from kindergarten to university. Does this man believe the quality of his brain which earned him a degree in another man's culture is inferior to the Caucasian American who cannot even speak his language, let alone earning a bachelors degree in any human academic discipline in his culture, among his people?

But, It Is Okay

The Africans I am talking about in this book are Africans in the African continent and other African descendants living outside the continent. I regard African Americans living or trapped in the US as Africans in this book. I also regard Africans and West Indian Africans living in Europe and in Caribbean Islands as Africans in this book.

I also recognize there are, especially among Africans, "African Americans" of Negroid descent, but have one of their parents as European Americans. Such Africans resent being referred to either as "African Americans" or "Africans." Instead they choose to be referred to as Irish, Scottish, Italian, Danish Americans. That is okay. I have no quarrel about such individuals. I am not addressing such individuals in this book. Their reason or reasons for their claim is okay with me.

My reason for addressing both Africans in the African continent and Africans outside the continent is that the pattern of corruption in African communities is the same. Espionage into corruption in this book is the same in Nigeria, Congo, Algeria, Egypt, Zimbabwe, Kenya, Ethiopia, Tanzania, the US, England, Haiti, or Jamaica. What I saw and wrote about in the *Sun Report* in the early 1970s among Bay Area African Americans and what I saw in Nigeria have striking similarities.

Economic progress in African countries is stagnant. This is okay. This makes Africans wherever they are ready consumers for European and US industrial products. This is okay, too.

Africans are not able to do anything for themselves, so it is okay for them to depend on the European and US businessmen–prostituting themselves as their errand boys. It is okay for African presidents or heads of state to be European and US errand boys. There is no reason why they should subject Africans to European and US wrath.

It is easy to perceive what the European and American god has done for them. He led them into economic adventures in Africa. He led them to enslave and colonize Africans. He leads them to decide both political and economic fates in Africa. All these are okay.

Democracy is okay in Africa. Is it not democracy that led Alexander the Great to conquer the ancient world—the Greek Empire? The same democracy built the Roman Empire, British Empire, and is modeling and creating the "twenty-first century" world for the US. This democracy is okay, too. It is okay for the Africans to mutilate their human dignity by frying their hair to change the texture, so that its "kinky" (American society's mocking word for the wooly nature of the negroid hair) quality of the same negroid hair is changed to the straight "animal" (dog, horse, or pig) nature of the Caucasian or Mongoloid hair. And bleaching their natural brown or charcoal color of their skin, changing their skin color to beige or orange skin color of Caucasian or Mongoloid? These are okay, too.

Some African Americans loathe their US (English or biblical) names. So they decide to change their names to "African" names and end up naming themselves Islamic names. This is okay, too.

No, It's Not Okay

What do all these have to do with corruption in African countries? Well, it appears I have talked myself into a corner. I do not really think so. At the same time, I am not a psychologist. But common sense tells me all these–democracy, wearing slimy hair, or bleaching the skin, shaving the hair, and becoming a Christian–fall into the African cosmetic things which make them acceptable candidates for European errand boys, either as business contractors or political agents as African presidents and their state commissioners.

This is what I am saying. Patrice Lumumba was not a good candidate for Congolese president in Congo, or Europe or US recognition either, because both European and US democracy did not impress him; even his plan for the Congolese was so good that US and European self-appointed "world political bosses" allowed General Mobutu to adopt the plan with a brand of democracy that kept him Congolese president for *thirty-five* years.

The snake which bit Lumumba in Congo scotched General Soni Abacha in Nigeria. He, too–like Lumumba–had nothing to do with European and US world political bosses and their democracy. He was branded a dictator and blacklisted and was assassinated for being Nigerian President for only *three* years.

Hosni Mubarak of Egypt was a good candidate for Western and US democracy in Egypt because he is their "errand boy" in the Middle East. Well, his brand of democracy has kept him in office as president of Egypt for *fifteen* years. *He is not a dictator.*

It is not okay to watch African economics, for years after the political independence of the 1960s, being stagnant. Africa is enviously located at the richest part of the earth. The tropics endow the continent with rich vegetation and soil. Still the economics of all the countries in the continent is stagnant.

The geological makeup on the continent blesses Africa with rich minerals, yet the economics of the countries in the continent is stagnant.

No, it is not okay to watch Africans as consumers of European and US industrial products, products which are from of the raw materials from Africa. Imagine Nigeria producing millions of barrels of crude oil every day in the year and having to import the same oil from Europeans and the US. No, it is not okay watching African economics being stagnant. It leaves negative feelings among Africans. It assaults their morals, and it abuses their human dignity. It reduces them to *Homo sapiens* who distrust their God-given human qualities.

It makes the African lose perception of who he is and forces him to mutilate the Negroid qualities that distinguish him from not only the human races but throughout the mammalian kingdom. Most Africans, especially the American breed, bleached their skins in a self-deceiving ambition to make themselves Caucasians while the Caucasians engage themselves in meaningful adventures to darken skins.

Most of the Africans fry and color their hair to make slick hair out of the crisp ginger Negroid black hair. Some even shave their heads to get rid of the Negroid hair. In the US this has recently turned to a male fashion, in that other races are now shaving their hair.

Nothing African is good for the conventional Africans. Their very beings as *Homo sapiens* in the human race is not good for them. Their gods are no divine beings but devil incarnate idols. So they wage wars against them, their lives, the very conscience of their land, and their very beings!

This is the beginning of the espionage into corruption in Africa because such hideous social activity as Western economics and political activities demand humans without conscience.

Conventional Africans agree with Europeans and the US that their (African) societies are savage and therefore have no political system. Africa from Cape Town to Tripoli, Nigeria to Kenya, Tanzania to Senegal have savage social systems, therefore no political systems. These conventional Africans therefore mortgage their political systems for European and US democracy.

The faceless Athenian political system which allowed only adult males to decide the political and economical systems among their people is now the US arm bolt and police state political system being imposed on Africans with the African academic and political elite as the agents. No, it is not okay to watch the South African president participating in the assassination of Nigerian political elite and hawking Nigeria—a country of one hundred thirty million Africans—for the best bidding in the Western World. I wonder what went on in Libyan Muammar Kaddafi's mind as he embraced President Mubarak of Egypt, as they hugged each other as brother presidents of African land!

No, it is not okay watching this Western democracy (Western or European) enslave Africans in a slave trade which lasted for more than three hundred years and cost African countries millions of lives. No it is not okay knowing the US developed the Japanese economy–Japan, a country with no natural resources–into what it is today, that it sometimes threatens the stability of the US economy with this democracy by transferring technology from the United States to Japan. With the same democracy the US enslaved Haiti–a country without natural resources, like Japan–and left the country as the world's poorest and US industrial consumer. It is not okay to know that this democracy is a European and US cosmetic designed for peddling mindless European and US capitalism in Africa. It is not okay watching Africans committing genocide on themselves with espionage into corruption in the name of this democracy.

Observation

I started writing this book when I was an administrator at Benin-City at the Institute of Continuing Education in Bendel State, Nigeria–that den of evil– and that was twenty-two years ago. It was actually thrilling and sad to watch espionage into corruption in action at the institute. I felt like a student (after writing *The Lost Totem of the Cheerful Savage* in 1976) coming out of my lectures on theory of corruption in Africa, only to enter the laboratory for the practical knowledge at the institute.

I was aware of the corruption network in Kenya, that private farm of the African Burning Spear; Jomo Kenyatta; Liberia, the African country which parades that godfather William Tobman, who ran the country into a slum; Ethiopia, that ancient land of the Kush; and Meroe, which Haile Selasie ran into a nation without hope. When I see Ghanaians dodging immigration officers in Nigeria, and some ignorant Nigerians abusing their human dignities, my mind goes back to the sing-songs on Kwame Nkruma's nationalism and all he did for Ghana and Africa. How can a house built on a strong foundation fall? How strong was the foundation Nkruma built in Ghana? Was it not the same Nkruma whom the same Ghanaians attempted to kill several times and finally ran out of Ghana? I submit that the now acclaimed African nationalist Kwame Nkruma, like any African leader of his time, maintained a system of espionage into corruption. I wonder how African political leaders use democracy to mask their created monarchial thrones as presidents. Democracy is not African. It was Athenian, then Roman, then British, and later American. And in America, it is now a self-centered, gun barrel, wealth protectionist democracy. Of course there are the Eastern European types.

I wonder how and where democracy bred monarchies in these countries that they are so effective in their national politics as to breed the African presidents who are now life presidents. They all use espionage into corruption to breed and maintain their life presidencies.

Yes, I was saying that I found myself in a laboratory for practical experience in espionage into corruption at the Institute of Continuing Education, Benin-City. I found myself standing bare-footed in a den of snakes and trying to kill them without a machete, gun, bow and arrows, or even charms. And I was not in possession of the biblical Daniel's faith in his god or his spiritual power while in his lion's den. I was, and still am, just plain Echezonam, always trying to catch the wind with my naked hands.

The snakes in the den reared their ugly heads with demons in their eyes and spat out their venoms at me. It burned. It was deadly. It nearly robbed me of my dear life. Then I turned around and fled. But the roads–Nigerian social roads–were trapped with thorns, stinging plants, and insects. There were vampires also on the nation's ill-fated roads. The thorns pricked my feet. The plants and insects stung me, and the vampires went on and on, with ceaseless overtime sucking my blood. It is a mystery to me how and why I am still alive. Believe it or not, I am still very much alive and kicking.

I started this book as a result of my experience in the institute. The experience was the same as the library experience I had when I was writing *The Lost Totem of the Cheerful Savage*. Then when I found myself holed up in Kano, *Espionage into Corruption* revealed itself to me. Then I wrote *The Political Evil Wind*, a book on the cause of the ills in Nigerian politics. I wrote *Attainment to Humanity*, *Steps to Humanity*, and *Road to Revolution: Nigerian Police*. I tried to capture the fears, dreams, and hopes of a man in the streets of Kano, Lagos, Los Angeles, Berkeley, New York, London, Paris, Malmo, Tokyo, Bombay, etc., as the world's "globe trotter"–a nickname for me from the world press.

I had finished *Espionage into Corruption* at the institute. It was a one hundred page manuscript, not typed. I decided to read through it and have it typed–that was about two years later. Then I discovered I had written only the skeleton of the book. The book needed flesh to help my readers find where to grab it. Still the flesh does not make the book supple, plump, or pleasant to ears or eyes, because it is an exposition of the social evils and how they are manifested in Africa.

I had time at Kano to read the daily papers and watch the academic elite talking from both sides of their mouths on how to right the wrongs in Africa, only as a way to invite themselves into their nations' politics and governments. Then came the politicians with their lies–playing on the people's emotions, making themselves opulent on the people's resources, while they leave the people in want, squalor, ignorance, disease. I at the same time watched the businessman blindly strangle himself in his ambition to cheat the people. The student was a mess. He passed his tests by politicizing the system. It was sad to watch the quality of youth in him destroyed. The

African youth destroyed? The youth who developed into the African who built the Africa I described in *The Lost Totem*?

Yes, that African youth: He is nothing less than a swindler, drunkard, drug-addicted disco head and sexual maniac.

The most awful sight is to watch the conventional African woman. I called her the "Bottom Power" in the book. She is the heart of the social sin in Africa. The ambition of every woman–any woman–is to look for and acquire a husband. The conventional African woman's ambition is to search for money, and she is ready to do anything–I mean anything–to get the money without sweat. She is a sex maniac. She is a drug addict. She is a child-killer. She is an animal without heart. She is the devil incarnate. She is a bag of disease. Her beauty and seductive smiles, swaying buttocks, looks, etc., are fast-acting poisons that kill the insects which visit the inviting flowers.

The aim of the book is an attempt to reveal how espionage into corruption in Africa is carried on the Africans and its ugly effects on Africa and Africans. Self-preservation is the first law of nature; it is the same thing to Africa. But the African of yesteryear had developed the culture of live and let live. The modern African has developed the conventional culture of individualism, and flowers into wars of disguising it in other isms: socialism, communism, capitalism. It is this disposition which makes the conventional African a cutthroat social monster. He searches for the easiest ways to exploit, cheat, or rob his neighbor so as to maintain a higher degree of fleshly comfort.

The conventional African is the prisoner of his conscience, that is if it were assumed he had any. He deliberately talks–in fact, preaches–of virtues, but lives in vice, still preaching the same virtue with no shame at all. Then when he is caught in the net of his sins, crimes, and lies, he blames others. He calls them bourgeois, capitalists, communists, traditionalists, reactionists, socialists, chroniclers, etc.

It is easy to observe that a people who live in self-deceit must wind up in self-destruction. This is not mere prophecy. It is just that anyone who listens to the African social elite talking, and at the same time watching him in his vice, must know that his future is bleak and that the African is in actuality inviting the calamity on himself and his society.

The conventional African parades himself as a politician, farmer, businessman, engineer, educator–name it, he is that–but he is none in reality. He is only a devil to himself and his society.

Fear often grips weaklings like me watching the modern African in his espionage into corruption, cutting the fibers which hold Africans together as people. How and where can one talk about or observe decency in Africa? In Cairo, Lagos, Dakar, Dar-re-Salaam, Kampala, or Accra, etc.? Decency in the streets or in the societies? Decency in Africa belongs to yesteryear and has been nicknamed old fashioned, ancient, archaic, and uncivilized in conventional Africa. And the African does not feel good any longer. Conventionalism does not and cannot control his problems. Sleep runs away from him, and he is tense. Food becomes the luxury he can afford but dare not take because he lacks the appetite. The evil network of his society makes drugs available to relax him. It is no use. Still no food, no sleep. He is still tense, and he seeks relaxation in excitement in corruption, for it offers him false exaltation in ill-acquired wealth and position. The conventional African cannot seek for excitement in creative activities because he lacks the skill, patience, and vision. He is crafty, all right, so he relies on rote while pride denies him practice through practical work. He is an expert in theory, and he does well in his armchair as an egocentric philosopher.

Here lies my fear for Africa, for this land of our heritage is now in the hands of egocentric armchair philosophers. It hurts to see Africa the way I see it, for it continually eludes me how Africans can assume their rightful place in the society of man with people who glorify themselves in self-deceit and self-destruction. This is the reality in Africa: Africans living in filth, sin, crime, and downright dirt.

This assault on Africa by Africans is lamentable. Had these Africans been aliens to the land, I could have entertained the hope that one day—one glorious day—the gods of the land will run them out as they ran out the colonists.

But again, here mounts my fears. Our gods do not and cannot run their children out of the land of their heritage. The gods usually pinch their ears to make them listen. If they remain deaf, the gods are decent beings and cannot tolerate filth, sins, and lies. Their wrath is usually the last solution. Their wrath is not selective as the angels selected Lot from the biblical Sodom and Gomorrah. Ah, me. And I have always tried to be like the gods. But the sad destiny of fate leaves me among the weeds. Even the weeds are already taking care of my dear life, before the wrath from the gods.

I feel this way because the wrath is not discriminatory. Once it is set off, its mission is total. It provides no shelter for individuals.

How can a person who wrote *The Lost Totem of the Cheerful Savage* wait helplessly for the predicated wrath from the gods? How can one watch the wrath devour such a heritage as is shown in the *Attainment to Humanity*? The thought leaves me feeling like a foreigner in the land of my birth. In fact I feel like I am losing my sanity whenever I realize that, whatever I think, I am the same African as any African of my time—the conventional African. Well, I am, but I am not proud of the conventional Africa which has draft-ed me into its cult. Maybe I am not that African, and this thought, though deceitful, is consoling. It leaves me and many other Africans like fish out of water, and nobody cares.

Africans have grown insensitive to corruption and its vice, and thus have lost their glorious heritage, lost their dignity, and may be losing their posi-tion in the society of man, and contain themselves in hustling and living in illusion. Yet they know the life they created in conventional Africa is a deteriorating life which will eventually lead to death and extermination.

The illusion of wealth is deceitful. Nature made the African an enviable being. His very personality is imposing. His heritage is divine, and therefore that makes him godly. His environment is the richest spot on Earth. But when they take to corruption, the gods desert them, leaving them in sin. They have taken to the new isms which have conditioned them to become mindless, insensitive, and cutthroat negotiators. If you put two Africans in a room, once they can communicate fairly well, you have got a political party. If you put three of them in a room, you've got a revolution or a business corporation. Both the politics and revolution revolve around money, sex, drugs, and all other social vices. They call it "business."

These Africans are soundly very serious when they talk about concern for their society and mankind. They are naturally cheerful and can pretend to be interested in the peoples' affairs. They do all these as invitations to get themselves into the lives of the people; then all of the sudden (after they have got the confidence of the people) they become different beings, and the only thing they have in mind is the exploitation of the people they used to build themselves. They, in fact, abuse the people's human dignity and, in most cases, kill them.

What these conventional Africans do does hurt. It hurts so that one does want to skin them alive. But how can an idle gossiper like me "bell the cat"? Where do I start? With whom do I start? The destiny of Africa and posterity hangs hopelessly over a bomb with its fuse dangerously close to naked fire.

With *Espionage into Corruption*, which is the naked fire, the bomb is sure to blow up and the destiny of Africa and her posterity may go in flames. This is no idle gossip. The conventional African elite have no time to think of destiny and posterity. These two words are flowery and lofty. Still, they see the sad result of their politics and revolutions. They see society go up in flames and know that it takes centuries to build societies. The signs of their savage claws are everywhere in the African society of our time. Their actions are crippling Africa, and nobody cares. I have read about these freaks. I have seen them. I worked with them at the institute. And I have lived with them. They are weak little fellows. They lack initiative. They have no skill. They are afraid to take risks. They are not adventurous. One does not like such freaks. You despise them, because they are of no good. One cannot relate to them, because they are evil.

I wonder, and seriously wonder, how the Africa that produced Uzu Aguokei, Chaka the Zulu, Herbert Macauley, Lumumber, Odimegwu Ojukwu, Oba Akenzua II, Ben Bela, Augusto Neto, Sadat, Unobueze, and a host of others produced such freaks who are the conventional African elite. There must be something wrong somewhere, for I still believe that Mother Africa, with all her motivations, daring, and divinity, cannot be responsible for such freaks. It makes no sense to regard such sub-humans as human beings. They are murderers, arsonists, saboteurs of progress, enemies of humanity. One loses track of all the evils they are and can create. They are poisonous and infectious. They are robots–mindless and insensitive–following orders, asking no questions, and living like rats in the darkness and fear. It appears they live in opulence, but they know inside themselves they own nothing. They are so hypnotized by such a dirty life no one can talk to them about the evil they are causing to themselves and to Africa and Africans.

Still, when I see these conventional Africans, my mind reverts to what Africa was and for what it stood. Today Africans who never knew fear live in fear in the land of their birth. It is painful to watch Africans who were born as intelligent, dynamic, imaginative, colorful, persistent, and friendly people turn into insensitive brutes. Africans are basically proud people who have respect for labor and human dignity.

But these packs of murderers are the contemptible death squad which is killing the best of us day after day and controlling Africa today. You see them as little gods in corners of the continent, causing troubled waters and fishing in them.

These tin-gods run the scarlet thread of the network of bribery and corruption in the African public life. The horror of their activities in Africa is unimaginable. They are the core of the evils in Africa. They are the financial buccaneers who use public service in the adventure of soul-destroying in Africa through pervasive, petty, corruptive activities and cynical corruption of the influential. They have successfully engulfed the statesmen, the police, civil servants, politicians, administrators, commissioners, governors, clerks, typists, messengers, etc.

These are the able men who run African countries. They are all corrupt with wealth acquired at the sacrifice of public conscience and the culture of the land.

It is hard to tell Africans about what they know of themselves. Words and phrases are wrapped in the cocoon of ambiguity for anyone who speaks or writes on the open secret. The core of the matter is that Africans like me choose to blame colonialism for wrongs we do to ourselves. Still, it is now history that the 1950s and '60s created the wind which blew away colonialism from Africa, leaving pockets of it among Africans that have developed in the evils and corruptions in both high and low places in African societies.

The sum total of individuals' illicit gains is the larger scale corruption and inefficiency now strangling the Africans, leaving them helpless in the ugly claws of man's inhumanity to man. It is depressingly mean and squalid to watch corruption grow robust and buccaneering standard. Its effect is pervasive, loathful, and disheartening. The stark reality is unpleasant.

Corruption has so engulfed the Africans that they, too, encourage the cancerous worm in their conspiracy of silence. Africans are by nature friendly and cheerful people–but not the conventional African. He is a corruption-hardened man. He is out to exploit his neighbor corruptively and can only trade his cheerfulness and friendliness for illicit "dash," percentages, or fleshly comport.

These Africans are a group of unhappy looking people. They look as if they are waiting for the gallows. But their sadness, in a way, is a put-up show, waiting for bribery of any kind. What has happened to the carefree, happy, and ever-friendly African? He has been seduced by espionage into corruption.

Initiative and creativity among these Africans are dead. They are not interested in creative and productive work. The work is only a front gateway for their illicit activities. Their ambition is focused on how many souls they have wrecked with their insensitivity and callousness in a day. Life for a conventional African is a dead-end street. The conventional African has turned things which make life interesting and stimulating into instruments they can use to suppress the Africans and control their corruption network. These Africans are dead hands. You get nothing but old, trite interests in them. Extortion, intimidation, and gangsterism are their versions of progress, concern, and development. These Africans are confused, and their lives are mingled with horror and hopelessness. This is sad and tearful, because they infest such horror and hopelessness throughout Africa.

The true smile of laughter that comes from the heart, that the African is known for, now eludes him. The conventional African does not have such a smile of laughter. What you see in their staged laughter or smile is pity and confusion. I consider such Africans as sub-humans, for their activities work against their security and future welfare. They appear to understand this, because they are very bitter. It is dreadful to know how bitter they are. They worry all the time about their security, for they are closer to death than any other being on earth. They live in fear. Yet they disguise their feelings in deceit and the pretence of made-up happiness and ill-acquired wealth.

It is mournful that these Africans are tearing down the fibers which hold African societies together without any hope of rebuilding what is being torn down. They have a barbaric custom, which they clothe in their modern social isms and guard with their lives. The isms are, of course, their lives, because they clothe their weakness and insatiable desires and greed and leave them to simple-minded Africans as sheep bleating for better ways to better the lives of the mass. Attempting to come closer to the sheep, one finds the sheep are savages in sheep skins. These savages take delight in causing disappointments, heart breaks, failures—events of misfortune for the curious Africans who dare come closer to the sheep to ascertain the authenticity of the sheep. These Africans are dangerous because they hurt the progress of Africans and undermine their destiny.

Human nature is funny and may be wicked, too, when one takes a close look at the aura of excitement. Thinking about it, and in fact observing it, it seems fragile and of limited appeal. The men in the game are heartless men, swatting their way through African social lives. They are for nothing but the commands and pleasures of their godfather.

The espionage into corruption is depressing, seductive, and satanic. It is a game of life with hidden cruelty and basically ruthless. Its activities are spiteful, and only the egg-headed Africans who lack creativity, skill, ambition, self-assurance, and security are easily seduced. It baits them with nectar, and when trapped, any attempt to escape means death. They are plagues to the African youth and women. I see them as little children waiting for their parents, then some jesters appeared playing sweet music, and the children leave the security of their homes and dance along after them, far away into seduction into corruption. That is the land of sin and crime. It is a land of free sex, alcohol, drugs, blackmail, prostitution, intimidation, murder, arson, armed robbery, bribery, "ten percent," godfathers, and evils. It is a land that conventionalism has created in the heart of Africa.

The elite of seduction into corruption are the ones who have the courage to break the traditions and perpetuate their actions by legalizing them. Look into the constitutions in Africa, and you will know what I mean, who wrote them, and why they wrote the constitutions as they are. And when the constitutions clash with the culture of the people and the controls go off balance, they disappear into Western and Eastern worlds on self-imposed exile, still living in opulence, and continue staging a comeback into the countries they ruined. They are usually successful in coming back and are able to set the espionage into corruption in motion again and continue bullying the Africans on whom they have diplomatically imposed themselves. These Africans have brutalized their neighbors into a mold in which they give it right back to the weak ones, who in their turn expand the mindlessness to still the weaker ones to them. Thus Africa, the home of humanity, returns to a jungle of the survival of the fittest. This is the conventional Africa with the mentality of never escaping from the whole filthy mess of seduction into corruption.

Human dignity on the basis of self-identity, which African culture bestows to the sons of the land, disappears at the arrival of espionage into corruption. Thus Africans now exist in pockets of categorized human beings. This is a mockery of nature, because as espionage into corruption strives to change the African, the sun still shines, the rain still falls, the vegetation still blossoms, the beautiful birds still sing, the butterflies still flout the air and visit pretty flowers. Africa is still consciously gay while the human beings, the creations of the gods, are rotten—rotten because they have been seduced into sin and crimes by the conventional African social elite with espionage into corruption.

When I think of what Africa is and what Africans were, the conventional Africa and Africans are like beings in a bed of roses and melodious music, floating through ugly-smelling cities and murdering humanity. It is hard to forget the mundane life in Africa which is run through espionage into corruption.

It is easy to forget the pain from a wound, but what the pain from the wound has done to Africa and Africans through espionage into corruption may never heal, thus the pain equally remains so.

It is not a pleasant thought for me to know I am an African of the conventional era. But here I am, an African of the conventional period. I often obsess with the thought that Africa is a continent where the stars are always bright. I always think of Africa and Africans as the star, like the diamond in the sky which will brighten the world.

Then some of the conventional Africans with their espionage into corruption cover the diamond in the sky with a very dark cloud. The twinkling little stars are now covered with clouds, and life and living have become an illusion. They cannot even brighten themselves; how can they brighten the world?

Maybe it is not reasonable for me to write these types of books. But the thoughts continue haunting me, and peace continues to elude me until I pick up my pen to scribble my feelings. I found out that the more I resist the urge to express my feelings, the more I am able to evade the truth I must face eventually. But what truth? Some force propelled me to Kano and told me in my dreams to visit a political party's office, which led to my writing *The Political Evil Wind*, and with the remainder of my research notes, I wrote *Road to Revolution: Nigerian Police.*

No voice spoke to me or is speaking to me to write *Espionage into Corruption*. It is simply an urge I am unable to repress. I am glad, though, that I am a being who never debates with himself, if the "ugly" self's dictations are to my understanding for the good of man. It relieves me to think thus; the thought energizes me to face the odds, and the odds are not beautiful. They are always horrors, never compassionate and always mindless. I hate the odds, and at times I hate myself for embracing them. I sound melodramatic. Well I have to, for I live in melodrama.

Echezonam, living in melodrama? Could this be tension and frustration forming a hideout where violence lurks in the shadows? Could it be fear of having my will to live—the will to be absorbed and paralyzed, my conscience stifled until hate was born—strong and eager? But I have conditioned myself not to hate, because hate is the ugly urge that quests feverishly toward destruction. The welfare of the society of man dominates my feelings for hate, and I find myself hating evil, for it is evil to hate.

History will not forgive the conventional Africans because of their assault on the human dignity of Africans. They made them fools who are absent-minded, who may continue forever to search for their destiny, whereas they hold their destinies right there in their hands.

Africans were firm in what they were before the strange modern Africans polluted them and poisoned their societies with espionage into corruption. Now Africans—the heirs of our fathers—are a pliable and submissive fools, totally immature and undeveloped.

I find it natural for me to be in a state of shock, knowing what I know about Africa. It is a shameful kind of shock that, instead of telling the world how good and lovely Africans and their Africa are, I seem to find delight in washing my people's dirty linen in the public.

I cannot call my birth with such destiny as mine a successful adventure. But here I am knowing that and that makes my adventure on Earth unbearable, and I yet find my hands so tied I am unable to do anything about it. There may be millions of Africans in the same shoe with me. We are only left, not even to follow our destiny, but to grope in an unidentified, instinctive illumination which leads to nowhere.

It is painful to know what you are and yet at the same time to let your neighbors treat you as if you were rubbish. They know you know they are inferior to you. Believe me, no one likes that, and still it happens to the Africans who snob espionage into corruption as a social leper. It is a sad destiny to be born in the conventional Africa and now know what to expect. Maybe this book may serve as a pilot to posterity, or stir up conscience to eradicate this cancerous system of espionage into corruption, and recreate a pure cradle of independence for every African. It is sad to watch Africans, true sons of the land, behaving like fugitives from justice in the land of their birth. The horror and distaste of the fate of such Africans can and never will outweigh any discretion, because the horror is haunting. It allows no room for anyone's relaxation or intentness. An analysis of such feelings reveal the continuing invasion of the horror created by the social systems designed by espionage into corruption in an indescribable atmosphere. The horrors are practical. They are visible; they are distasteful and murderous. They are the horrible kind of horrors. Such horrors make one a stranger in the silence they create. They make Africa a haunted place and menacing for Africans.

Espionage into corruption is not an imaginary social system. It exists. It asserts its presence. It succeeds to have its ways, which are usually impositions to the people. One does not say no to its agents. To say no means death–a fast or slow one. One does not have to scream or put up a fight against such monsters, for there are no rescuers from the conventional Africa. The approach is submit or die, and many choose to submit. The few who choose to put up a fight die in their attempts or take to their heels after a time of fruitless struggle against the heartless monsters. Living with the agents of espionage into corruption is rough and deadly. One finds himself facing and struggling with life with emptiness, motivated only by the will to live. The agents are spoilt and indulging beyond anyone's wildest dreams. Their genius is for intimidating and plaguing poor and underprivileged Africans. They are the images that represent money, comfort, and carefree life without any corresponding obligations or responsibility. They are therefore more than painful. Africans are in despair. They pretend to be in pain and more from the reality of the pains in growing nations into dormant developments of non-productive citizens who can only consume to maintain other people's economics. This dormancy of non-productive economics is worsened by being saddled with dens of corruption which have taken time to build a permanent home among Africans. This is the despair in which African nations have found themselves. It is, of course, frustrating, and these Africans believe they can run away from the frustration and hope to find relief in alcohol, sex, violence, etc. Funny, and sadly funny, Africans have turned themselves into killers of others and themselves, and such uncontrollable methods of mass self-destruction are the ugly fate which threatens Africa as a nations and race of people or nations of men.

Africans never learn from the past; instead they choose to challenge the events of yesteryear and deceitfully pretend they have defeated the native and its history. Even as they pretend in their world of self-deceit, they watch themselves waste away slowly into national decay. Corruption has struck African rights with violent deaths and loose sex among undisciplined youth who support themselves with Indian hemp and drugs from underground world. Corruption now walks around the African's homes, schools, establishment, streets, market places, etc., with a knife-edge of horror and excitement and no difference between the Africans who are struggling to build their nations and the destroying Africans whose interests are mainly to satiate their immediate selfish ends. This is the African. The sole beast divided within himself.

Why are Africans what they are today? Why have they chosen this way of life? Or did their gods make them the downtrodden human beings reeling under the heavy burden or continuously sustaining the few wealthy Africans in their corruption rings?

It is shameful to stand aside and see Africa as it is and believe the ugly reality that you, too, are an African belonging to a people of one of the nations that have boundless potential and still are doomed to never realize his destiny—only to remain a race that kills ambitions, a race that kills her own children! Africa works overtime to discourage any hard-working African in both public and private establishments. The establishments, even the public, are showcases which cover up the underground trafficking of business. Hard work reveals the officers who sit behind their large tables on their swivel chairs waiting for instructions from the underworld who really install them in the establishments as executive officers, assistant secretaries, commissioners, directors, chairmen, etc.

A handful of assistant secretaries and executive officers once advised me in an establishment for which I was working that I did not have to work hard. I told them I knew I was underemployed, that they had been frustrating me in the establishment, but I had convinced myself no one person can clean the corruption in Nigeria, and that the only way to make things work in Nigeria is through hard work. This reply was disappointing to them. A few days later all of them conspired to make life miserable for me, and when I ignored them, they removed the schedule from me and left me redundant. Still I created assignments for myself, at the same time facing them squarely by raising petitions on their maladministration at misusing of public funds.

This stirred up the bees in their nest. All the other establishments and secret societies ganged themselves against "poor" me, a lonely African who now hates his nationality.

The nonsense of bringing our children back home from the Western nations to help develop Africa is a mere propaganda of the self-stifled "nationalists" who portray themselves with that air of importance and not believing themselves, and at the same time want no one around them to challenge their authority. Nationalism is dead in Africa; only the nationalism that gives allegiance to the corrupt world is not only in full strength in the continent, it is conversing for members and is quickly converting the academic elite into their world of sects in the forms of clubs which replace the secret societies in Africa, made up of nations that are wrecked, crude, filthy, and polluted, a cold prison cell for the honest, hard-working, and ambitious Africans, where they eventually perish or be seduced into corruption. Africans have turned their countries into a miserable world, and with their actions have made them miserable. They regard this as a new world of progress, nations that grow (not thrive) on sin and crimes. They believe they are conquering this new world by losing themselves in it, hoping to reap what they sowed—evil. They cannot reap anything but evil, for that is what they sowed.

One has to be inside Africa to know how this evil has eaten her down. Africans are cold, ruthless, and crude in their search for money. They stop at nothing in their adventure to acquire wealth. This is what they call success.

Race Without Dreams

There are no dreamers–the brooding, idealistic dreamers–among conventional Africans. They destroy dreams, and thereby strangle creativity, and replace it with cynicism–a cold and ruthless mad race for money, cars, and loose women, for concubines, wives, and schools of children who they do not have time to play with or supervise in their upbringing.

Their children grow up without direction. Many of them are unable to make it through the classrooms because they cannot conform to order. Just like their parents (order means control, and control means supervision), order is to be discouraged for it is a threat to corruption and therefore a threat to Africans.

Youths in any society are usually dreamers, and the world is built on dreams. African youths are no dreamers; they are pleasure seekers who hate themselves, their culture, their villages and homes. They are youths who have encouraged their parents to destroy their language and have voluntarily adopted the American ghetto language originated from the slaves' baby talk, trying to imitate their masters, which they make worse when they speak it with a funny accent. Conventional African youths are not adventurous like other youths. Their adventures are only into corruption, where the corruption dragnets lay in ambush, waiting to encourage them into their world. In fact the conventional African youth's ambition through the classrooms either in Africa or in the Western world from the high school to doctorate degree is the ambition of attempting to break the door to easy (cool) money and wealth, which the "system" with its arms of corruption had agreed to open for them.

No human society tolerates lawlessness, or if it tolerates it, it does not perpetuate it. But African societies are unique. They do not only tolerate it, they perpetuate it and fight the odds that may redirect it to sanity.

Conventional African societies are bad, societies that kill their children. They welcome the children from birth, brainwash them into destroying themselves, and watch them die prematurely—before attending to the old age. It is a tearful sight to watch innocent African children playing, only to realize that more than many of them may not die natural deaths.

Conventional Africans are a strange group of people. Their ambition to acquire the almighty money is one-track minded, and completely uncontrollable. To them, the end justifies the means. They believe in nothing but money, sex, cars, house, and children they hate to touch.

Nature has given African societies a very rich environment, and Africans have mortgaged this for corruption—corruption upon all evils to dominate the healthy minds of the youth. It is sad for Africa with corrupted youth, because she has no future as a race of people. Life had been fair to Africans, but they have chosen the devil for a bedmate. It is difficult to believe the African belongs to the animal kingdom anthropologists call *Homo sapiens.* He appears in the form of the "wise being" with large gray matter in his skull but does not behave like him or even organic matters who honestly respect the great law of nature, which states that the first law of nature is preservation of the species. These Africans belong to the human race but are no longer human. The corrupt espionage has claimed their souls and has turned them to human beings without souls—mere walking shadows.

Only in Africa can one hear that nature wronged Africans by having created them in tribes. Africans never cared to find why nature created them in tribes. Nature should have her reason, for the same nature created them and the water they drink, the air they breathe, and the seasons of the year which provide them the environment. There is wisdom in the creation of nature. Why do Africans not find wisdom in Mother Nature for creating them in tribes?

The adult now exploits tribalism, by using it as a political instrument to exploit the country against the interest of their nature and their people, and uses their secret societies to unify the country for their self-centered purpose, forgetting that nature had reason for creating Africans as they are.

The youths forget their tribes in their haste to become rich, right from the kindergarten playground to their big tables as secretaries, executive officers, or businessmen. Look at the Africans today. They look alike in dress; they sound alike in language.

They behave alike—the same acquisition tendency and ruthless pursuit for money, sex, tobacco, alcohol, corruption, violence, etc. This is the African youth—Hausa, Kikuyi, Ashanti, Yoruba, Wolof, Ibo, Zulu, Ga, etc. These are African nations. This is what Africa gets for destroying tribalism, for the tribes had been the schools which molded and controlled African behaviors.

Africans live in fear—the worst state a man can live in any human society. The fear is everywhere in the country. The child grows up in fear in his home, school, and society. His attempt to get out of the frightful world drives him to the genocidal world of African corruptions and their social clubs.

There is no way out of the system. There is no getting used to the system. To be used to the system is to accept it, and accepting the system is compromising the evils of corruption into the reigns of one's way of life. There is no opposition to the system, since the youths have been indoctrinated right from their homes. There is no difference between right and wrong, because the wrong dominates the right and eclipses it so completely that what is right does not exist in Africa and finds it very difficult to surface again in the continent. The hope to restore what is right lies usually with the youths, and the youths are hopeless.

Individualism

"To your tents oh Israel, what portion have we in David." This biblical quotation describes African societies of today correctly. Every African has taken to his own way like the early man trying to survive in the jungle alone. The only law he knows is the laws of the jungle, which is the "survival of the fittest." That means the survival of the fittest at the expense of the weak.

Group life has been destroyed among Africans. Africans have to fight all the time to suppress the rights of those who do not belong to their sects and to claim the rights from them. This gives them satisfaction, that they have taught a non-member of their sect a lesson by taking his rights and giving the rights to one of them or to the one they are planning to hook. Africans continue to fight even in their sleep as much as when they are awake. Even in their secret societies the fight continues, and its rule is based on self-preservation, then the preservation of the secret societies. If one refuses to fight, everyone spits on his face. Africans will not only spit on his face; they will rob and cheat him. Money is the African's best friend; with money they can buy their way. They can even buy someone to go to prison for them.

But all is not well with these Africans. Their blind obedience to the corrupt masters solves their problems temporarily. They have sold their souls to a corrupt world in their hurry to be rich. They now find themselves with impossible tasks which mean death for them if they fail to carry them out, and in carrying out the assignments, they also face death. They cannot refuse the assignment. Doing so also means death.

Then what next? Frustration moves in, for frustration is the next logical human condition. This frustration is the kind coupled with anger. Such anger that causes an unsteady throbbing of the heart, the anger that pounds the heart loud and harsh. Such frustration sets one to sit down and take inventory of his past, and this is where the African finds himself.

The frustration forces him to lose his happiness, and contentment, and laughter. The face turns to stone. He begins talking to himself and starts avoiding others. He begins to hate himself and the environment that brought him up.

More reaction comes in. The African feels alone and bitter. The world becomes a dark place–darker than it had ever before been. Before he had wanted to be rich fast, and the agents of corruption had shown him the way. Now that he has been doing impossible tasks which have been threatening his life, and backing out from the sect means biting the finger that feeds him, and his underground society does not take such action lightly.

Then he blames the rationalists that society dragged him into such ugly world. But his reason is vague; he, at the same time, realizes he wanted those things which dragged him into the underground world. The more he thinks of such things, the more his face becomes colorless.

These thoughts push him to realize his only escape from the underworld is to eliminate it. Eliminate the underworld? The thought alone frightens him. Eliminating the underworld sects would remove the pain and the unhappiness in him, but the thoughts doubled the pain and unhappiness. Now it becomes clear to him that his alternative, if he wants to stay alive, is to remain with his underworld sect and take life as he sees it–just as it comes, without questions.

But this thought is not comforting; rather it caused a hot wave of pain and hatred to rise in him and turns his eyes red. He sees the whole human race in a different view. He does not like how he sees man. He hates him now. This hate transfers him back to the stone age man. To hell with the world. Still this hatred does not solve the problem for him. It makes it worse. He wants something that can make him feel human, but to feel human in conventional Africa is to be childish, because the child, just before he is five, is the only human being in Africa. He cannot bring himself to face the reality of life, that is to be like a child, if the only comforting ambition he has had has been over laboring himself through savage societies or clubs. He still feels empty because he cannot be like a child. Then he takes the only road open for him, and that is the murderous savage road in the sinful criminal world they call modern Africa.

That is conventional Africa all right. Life still goes on, but for how long? Life is short for those who will die untimely–this very hour or minute–and completely uncertain for the rest who live only by pushing through, waiting for the uninvited time to come.

The savage African crowd is still moving, with her frustrated people living, laughing, cheating, witching, fighting, and killing themselves.

It is when these sad events are personalized in the country that one is aware this faceless crowd is made up of Africans who go to jails and die every day. The crowd never dies. It thrives and moves on facelessly and mindlessly. There are crowds in all human societies, but the African is mindless, only with the mission to kill her sons and daughters, and maim those it cannot kill. Crowds may be the same all over the world, but African crowds are made up of killers, pimps, prostitutes, dirts, rotten smells, stagnant gutters, flies, mindless and unmovable motor traffic, mindless civil servants, lying politicians, unconcerned parents, women's "libbers," sex maniac youths, armed robbers, etc.

Leadership and Africans

It is possible, or rather believable, for one to assume that Africans wish to have a good society—a society with good life. This wish is both abstract and subjective at the same time. My perception of what is or should be the moral standard in Africa is not abstract, but can be relative to what I perceive to be good, criminal, sinful, or bad. But the untimely and unnatural deaths of Africans of our time are facts. The reality of the deaths are not relative but positive perceptions. The bad roads, the smelling gutters, the dirty market stalls, the undisciplined youths, the mindlessness that dominates the nations, and many different forms of man's inhumanity to man in Africa are realities. So Africans' wish for a good life or good society, whatever forms they make it. It is a desire for a something better than what dominates and controls them as societies—the societies of sin that subject them to live in fear in the lands of their birth, societies that made them slaves to the faceless, unidentified, mindless underworld societies.

The good society that Africans are wishing for is that Africa which satisfies their basic psychological and social needs. Such an Africa should have a quantitative character as well as a qualitative one. The Africa they dream for must be better than the present African society and culture that are characterized with all the ugly forms of man's inhumanity to man where Africans are reduced to the untamed beasts of the jungle.

The society they are dreaming of is the Africa where a greater proportion of the populace shares in the good life. That Africa is yet to come—she is in the "Steps to Humanity," one of my unpublished manuscripts.

This good society can come, of course, only with the level of mores, which must have regard for the African "traditional cultures." This presents a good chance for Africans to have a common moral standard. But as long as African society is based on the exploitation of human nature for the benefit of the underworld societies, Africa must always remain a society of sin–the den of criminals.

A handful of Africans, usually those who have perfected themselves in the methods for exploiting human nature, have volunteered themselves as the African "Good Samaritans" with promises to lead the Africans to the land of milk and honey, to the underworld cultures of "man eat man" societies. These are the African leaders with their lofty promises of providing Africans good societies with a good life. Their leadership is the theme of this chapter.

Leadership is a position that the leader occupies combined with the quality of a leader. Such a leader must have the capacity–the ability to lead. He must be able to exercise the act of leading. He must be able to provide successful resolution of problems, must have the ability to mold individuals to form a team, and most essentially must direct the team to provide a "good life"–that is the salt in the "good society."

There has been leadership in Africa ever since the European colonists were run out of the continent and Africans assumed the leadership of the country. And look at what Africa is now! It is eerie to note the problems which engulf African leadership are the deficient ingredients of a leader.

Africans rightly removed the leadership positions from the European colonists, but these Africans lacked the ability to lead. They failed the nations because they were unable to exercise the ability to lead the nations. They lacked the act of leading their fellow Africans and therefore were unable to provide them with successful solutions for their problems and have failed to mold them as a team aimed at providing the "good life."

But why has African leadership failed so grossly and, in fact, so woefully? What are the qualities of a leader, and what are the qualities of African leaders?

There is no need to answer these questions. The most important is whatever the quality of a leader is, he should be accountable to the people he leads and must have the love and the interest of the people he leads at heart.

The African leaders do not love Africans and therefore do not have their best interests at heart. They are not accountable to Africans. They are accountable to the underworld sects that installed them as leaders with the mission to exploit and rob the Africans, then kill them when they resist. This is why African progress has become a merry-go-round in the world of disappointments and frustrations.

Still, there is a form of leadership in Africa. Who are the leaders? How do they lead and what are the outcomes of their leadership? They have turned Africa into a society of crime, sin, loose sex, drunkards, drug addicts, irresponsible citizens, and youths without futures.

They have turned Africa into a society of boodling; boodling should be treasonable and punishable by death, for political bribery is selling the nation for a mess of portage. Boodling is an accepted way of life in Africa.

Such prostituting of Africans' destiny does not cause any form of raised eyebrows in Africa. It is part of the disturbing theme of this book.

Africa is a nation of blackmailers. Blackmail is not even a crime in the continent. Blackmail to a people with moral principles is piracy. It is a way of life in Africa.

Embezzlement or "juggling the accounts" is theft. Embezzlement is robbing banks, stores at institutes, etc., with pens, as robbing banks, homes, and stores with gadgets or arms are crimes. There is no private office or public establishment in that continent free of embezzlement. Call it whatever you like. Embezzlement is theft.

Thanks to some military government for banning gambling and pool staking, but we know very well that both gambling and pool staking is well and alive in Africa and in fact is doing fine. The lottery is gambling, too, but since it is controlled by the government, it is all right. The effect is still the same.

How about taxation and its loopholes? Big business still dodges tax, and the underworld owns or controls big business. Larceny is a criminal offense and tax dodging is larceny.

Unemployment of fellow human beings is slavery. Exploitation of a fellow human being against his interest is equally slavery. African elite are not happy until they convince themselves that they have cheated or are cheating their fellow Africans. Of course, exploiting Africans is their assignment.

The African mass is becoming aware of what is "home made." They are characterized by their adulterations. Its economic impact to Africans is as criminal and sinful as murder.

Discrimination is a way of life in America. Africans only get ahead in their business or employment, private or public, if they belong to the right society, or they fall out of the line. Qualifications, hard work, and punctuality mean nothing to Africans if that African does not belong to the right group. That discrimination is not only a betrayal of trust; it is equally a criminal offense. Still, discrimination is a way of life in Africa.

All these actions: discrimination, unemployment, underemployment, tax-dodging, blackmailing, adulteration, and many other social ills are the conventional African way of life, which comes within the African scope of the law—the law notices them, and looks the other way. The law has been twisted to be an apparatus of the underworld. It has been twisted as a tool of the vengefulness of another. It is now a political gadget with which they run African societies. They have used it to bring the nations under their feet because politics has become a struggle of class against class while the mass is perpetually left in abject poverty and loss of human dignity.

Africans are aware of their suffering, but the business of keeping their flesh and bones together has not given them time enough to store up strong emotions on these cruel actions that African leadership inflict on them; and so they look at these social elite without letting loose the flood of wrath and abhorrence that they deserve for the long attended sins and crimes they have been committing against humanity and their fellow Africans.

African leadership does more harm in the countries than thieves or murderers. They earn their livelihood by menacing our treasuries and polluting the nations' ideals. The social elite own and control the banks where they borrow the money the oppressed mass earned from the corporations owned by the same elite, which they built with the mass sweat-earned income. Boy! It is a cutthroat world, and justice continues to elude the African masses. Why should justice not elude the African masses? Justice–fairness, reward of virtue, and punishment of vice, exercise of authority in maintenance of what is right–will tamper the rule of the game of the corrupt world. And they control the arms of justice anyway. So Africans are made to believe that they live under a government of law, while they are actually under the government of the underworld.

A friend told me that "time will change Africans." I'd like to believe that, I told him, but there was no way I could. I like to think of myself as a student of history, and history reveals that corruption existed as far back as when man started his first society, but corruption thrived in the human societies. Each society developed a gadget in the form of religion to check it by building and maintaining conscience in the minds of the citizens.

Corruption in Africa is a different case. It goes wholesale and really free wheel, with no religion to apply the break. The most effective religions are foreign–Islam and Christianity–and Africans are equally alien to them.

The only religion that is natural to them is nature worshipping, and the alien religions made sure they were relegated to the junkyards of the nations' antique.

Africans are therefore the same, with their varieties of crimes and sins, as the society changes or develops. Crimes have become industrialized as Africa develops into a modern world. Criminals have formed a corporate world to exploit the modern Africa. The chicken thief is now in an organized criminal. He does not steal chickens now. He organizes and carries out frauds in the banks and corporations. The criminal associations that have themselves installed in high places in the society offer him cover and protections.

The policeman is now his protector, the government provides him with a decent driver, too. The nation provides him judges and lawyers to supply moral interpretations of his actions.

These illicit actions are transcribed into books for children by their writers and printers and the administrators are bribed for the contracts to print them. Teachers are given commission (the notorious 10 percent) to approve such hideous sinful productions for African children to read and memorize to pass their examination.

Africa–a land so blessed by the gods that it is nothing less than the biblical "land of milk and honey"–is now importing the synthetic foods that are mass produced with drugs. The same foods could be produced by natural means in Africa, but that would deprive the underworld, the invisible government of the corrupt world, their commissions. So Africa loses the natural gift of assortments of food to the imported, drug-infested foods. Worse, African youths have lost the skill to farm the land and make it yield the abundant food nature had intended.

There was security in group life, but the underworld sects have so exploited it in Africa that society (group life) has lost its meaning and luster. African society now is a trap for the weak and opens doors for the wicked. African society puts Africans at one another's mercy and so allows the underworld the scope for more brutal activities against the African masses. An individual knows who is cheating him but cannot take legal action until there is buying and selling, and even with that the "screw up" of an individual is still difficult to dictate out, for the agents who are concerned in draining the life blood of the people have the skill of the trade against the interest of the simple-minded African masses.

The wage system is now used to keep Africans continuously as hired laborers, and the African social cannibals are now justified and rewarded by subjecting their actions to the judge.

African society now makes it possible for counterfeiting, speculations, treason, and smuggling. Their business world tempts the embezzler, the pirate, and the forger. This is what Africa now calls leadership of African society with their ruthless pursuit for private ends. Africans are the victims of their actions. They are used as pawns for the "business games."

The African masses are now very much aware that they are pawns in the hands of these boodlers, adulterers, and speculators, and while necessities of life allow them to subject themselves as pawns, they watch for a chance to join the nation's bootleggers; all these to the nation's misfortune. While the bloody criminals have spread to the African masses, the crime though is directed heartlessly to themselves and their national corporations. It is wrong to say that life goes on in Africa. A people without leadership cannot go on. It only waits to perish.

The arrogant bloody crimes of African leadership are not only the stealing and murdering of their subjects, but their boldness in the complexity of the African social relations are not actions carried at the dark corners and lonely streets of the nation's cities, and the midnight shows. They are actions that are more than night prowling, political negotiations, meeting at hotels, and simple instructions: "I don't care how you do it, but have it done." When this fails, the "jungle law" prevails. The jungle law that calls for the mugging and thugging. The jungle law that calls for transfers, withholding of promotions and entitlements, and when all these fail dismissal follows. And still, when this fails, then murder or their mysterious witchcraft.

Who makes up the African leadership? Who makes up these murderous social elite? They are the African covenant breaker, the subordinate witness, the corrupt judge, the oppressor of the poor and the underprivileged. They are the criminals in suits and traditional dresses. They are the bakers who knead chalk, alum, and plaster into the loaf of bread; they are those who adulterate the drinks and drugs for selfish profits. They are the figure jugglers in the establishment for selfish reasons in their ambitions to be rich fast; they are those who give okays to contract jobs only to recommend remodeling the same job a year later. They are the fearless criminals who are sure the law will vindicate them because they too can blackmail the judge if he fails to accept their actions as right in the eyes of the law.

African leaders are those who carry out their hideous bloody crimes believing that Africans do not notice their boodling is treason, that their blackmail is piracy, that their embezzlement is theft, that their speculation is gambling, that unemployment and underemployment are slavery, that mindless adulteration is murder.

They are therefore the Africans who destroy their fellow citizen's dreams and render them useless with their fraudulent actions. They are the Africans who grind the faces of other Africans on the tarred roads with their mindless monopoly. They are the Africans who destroy the African youth by exposing and indoctrinating the innocent minds to their illicit lives.

An ideal leadership should look at the productions of the citizens in terms of livelihood rather than profit and should therefore consider the social impact of the conduct. Their mission should be focused on the well being of their people instead of the selfish exploitation of their subjects.

But African leadership has no leaders. They are underworld spies in leadership's clothing. They are the errand boys of the corrupt world whose assignments are to exploit their brothers for cruel, heartless underworld sects.

African society is cheap and nasty. The public organs are aloof without dissection. The society, out of fear, condones such mindless cruelty from the underworld. The African mob, the pick pockets, shoplifters, such petty social deviants, beat them to death and tear down their establishments to build upstairs buildings and keep dozens of girlfriends. The nation's instinct of self-preservation has been destroyed by her lack of moral standard, which is the result of the lack of leadership. The leadership has led Africans to rob themselves with the method and standard of the notorious highway robber: "Your life or your money." But the victim in this case has a choice. He usually chooses his life, with the belief that, where there is life, there is hope to earn more money.

African leaders leading Africans to rob themselves in the highway style have destroyed the nations; no nation waylays her citizens at gunpoint and expects that nation to survive in the universe. This is the fate African leadership dangles over the nations, and conventional Africans are anxiously pulling down the fate, knowing full well that when it falls there will be no African nations, but hoping to escape the wrath by fleeing out of the country. God bless Africa. Why have the gods created such a people who enjoy killing their own children?

Africans have joined hands with their leadership to sell out their nations for money in exchange for poverty, squalor, filth, disease, stagnant traffic jams, mindless civil servants, fraud, commissions, etc.

Africans hate criminals, not in the sense of the danger of the crimes to their countries but out of sympathy for the victims. That is why African mobs take laws into their hands to punish the shoplifter, the driver who jammed somebody in the village, etc. The same Africans look the other way when they spot out the doodling speculation, adulteration, fraud, bribery, drug peddling, prostitution, and all other forms of illicit acts. To the Africans, any form of organized crime is acceptable. It is nobody's business.

Yet Africans are arrogant people. Listen to them outside their countries' borders. They tell the world how morality pants in its struggles to right the sinful world. They make the world feel ashamed of themselves, wishing to be Africans.

It is pathetic, sadly loathful to watch Africans talking from both sides of their mouths in telling the ignorant foreigners that cows in Africa have longer tails than their species all over the world. The same Africans are Africans they are. They know no shame. They are ready to digest the venom of their spleen, though it does split them for money or in search of vague prestige. But the world is not blind to the truth. Even the way the so-called rich Africans spend their money still describes them as idiots or fools trying to buy the prestige they are already abusing.

The same people they are trying to impress with their fingers laced with assortments of gold rings, two or three cars in their garages, big talks at the bars, bevies of girlfriends who would not mind sleeping with dogs for money, know how they made their money. They know they are the corrupt bosses who, in order to extort fat contracts for their companies, deliberately delay for months or even a year or more the building of a filtration plant designed to deliver the cities from deadly diseases, thereby subjecting thousands of people to early deaths.

The people these rich Africans are trying to impress in their laced robes know these Africans sacrifice their fellow Africans to the devils who sucked their blood and offer their bodies to diseases, who claim their share and surrender the rest to the grave. And so, one by one Africans march to their graves before their time, and their families mourn them and tearfully ask themselves why the gods let such evils come to them.

The rich Africans–the symbol of African leadership–have designed into their system the way the sinner, the criminal, is separated from the crime through a distant form of remote control. The duelers who were refused the ballot paper at the polls by a village of voters now use their remote control to withhold the road construction, power, water supply, etc. Contracts to the people: "Scratch my back with the ballot papers, and I'll scratch yours with these necessities." But this is not all. The contracts have been awarded and money spent on them. The rich Africans, the leadership, only write them off as bad debts while the people suffer.

The masses, being what they are, are blind. African masses–the unfortunate group is leaden with imagination. It is only moved by the concrete facts. The criminal usually escapes them, and in fact are adored and envied, but off sights the subtle iniquities that pulse along the viewless filaments of interrelation that bind them together–rich and poor as a nation.

How I wish that a Nigerian Murtala Muhammed were to appear in every nation in Africa on a goodwill mission to deal sternly with the duelers, the quack-doctors, the drug pushers, the contractors, the managers, directors, chairmen, commissioners, civil servants, the governors, the landlords–the African leadership. These African leaders escape the wrath of the masses because Africans squander the vitality of their anger on the old-style open air criminal who never looks his victims in the face as he strikes them.

That the nonchalant attitude of Africans over the crimes committed in their countries have led some of the nations into doom and may finally be on the way to finishing the job they started in the sixties, appears to be very clear. What is it that excites anger against these rich Africans? Is it the clash of capital and labor–the master and slave thing? The uncovering of the muddy source of the fortunes of these rich Africans? The hope of living on the crumbs of such illicit fortunes? The exposure of the rich Africans–the leadership who with their dirty money corrupt the nation's youth–as the captains on the African corruption liners? I mean revelation of the part they play, which is usually the business interests in the debauching of the nation, may be any of these, but the worst is the sufferings Africans go through because of these evil money grabbers and illicit pleasure seekers.

African leadership–these rich Africans, these illicit pleasure seekers, these corruption bosses, these invisible string pullers, these connection agents have wracked the social order in Africa. They have done and still are doing worse to Africans than harming particular individuals. They wound Africa itself. The Africans who steal elections, who bend the law to suit their purpose, who make justice a mockery, who pervert good custom, who foil the plain public intent, who pollute the wells of knowledge, who dim ideals for hire–these are the Africans in sober truth, the criminals and sinners, the African leadership. They are cutting the African beams that hold the roofs over Africans' heads as nations. They should be the first to feel the wrath that is descending on the nations.

To spare them because nobody can point a finger at them or stir an indignation is equally as criminal as the nations' leadership, because the nations will sink with her people, and that will be Africa's fate.

The complexity of African leadership is farmed in more ways. Africans see no crimes against their countries once no one is singled out. Even when someone is singled out, Africans quickly generate the feelings that "everybody does it" and go about negotiating the evils. And before one notices it, the criminal is initiated into the corrupt world, if he had not been a member before. Right from there, justice begins to elude its course until pressure is brought on the owner of the pointing finger to the criminal; and still, if the finger persists, the table is turned against the accusers and he may begin to be seen as the criminal. So the crime against the nations survives luxuriously, and this grows into habits of the leadership doing what they like and Africans letting them. This is treason in both ways. The leadership that stops approved contracts for supplying water, power, good roads, etc., should be hanged publicly. The leadership that delays or denies contracts or over inflates it in attempts of getting commissions of any percentage should be hanged publicly. The leadership that underemploys personnel or allows unemployment should be hanged publicly.

Stop and look at what I am saying. How much money have African countries lavished on these so-called educational programs, agriculture, health, welfare, roads, etc.? Billions, and you know what I mean—billions in hundreds and thousands, and Africa is worse than what it was. Where are the billions? In the African leadership purse. They control the percentages; they supply the materials for the projects; they are the contractors. They initiate and recommend the projects, and they fix the prices. God bless Africa! The poor Africans are the laborers, and these are the lucky ones. There are hundreds of ways in which Africans' common interests can be hurt, and every year finds them more vulnerable. Each national project draws African countries into a now dangerous zone.

African leadership's zealousness to grab the money often sacrifices the nations' social good and escapes as the nations' public enemies, because their crimes are directed to the African public and not to the African individuals. These actions of these mindless leaders stagnate progress and reduce the quality of human dignity in Africa to that of slaves. Nothing can check this creeping paralysis in the nerve centers of Africa but the unquestionable nationalism among Africans. But nationalism is completely absent in Africa. The professors, preachers and other "do-gooders" are equally in the money race to dupe the nation to fill their pockets. They, too, have betrayed their professions and the trust Africans have in them.

Leadership in Africa stinks. They exploit and feed upon the helpless, the dying, and even the dead. No wonder African millionaires sprung up out of the dead in the civil wars' fields.

The growth of crimes in Africa is the developing campaign to industrialize the nations. How many industries have been built in Africa since the campaign, and how many Africans have been absorbed or developed in these industries? The statistics do not have the data for the answer, because there are hundreds of industries in both paper records, and in reality and only tens of Africans have found jobs. Underemployment and unemployment are still at the point of slavery in Africa. The numbers employed are either through favoritism, nepotism, bribery, or tribalism.

Developing the nations are new gateways they have opened for their greed. This allows the creation of new industries that never solve the nation's economic problems, rather they make them worse. The reality of how they loot the nations is their method of operation.

The projects they thought out for developing African nations open the door to rob the nations of their wealth while Africans watch with opened eyes. They set to work with fake diplomas, false advertisements, and bogus testimonials. With these dealing instruments, they position themselves with their fake papers. They set up a medical center or hospital with the medical qualifications or print medical agents that takes care of the advertisements; next come the projects, or even setting themselves up can also be parts of the projects. From there on, it becomes a matter of transferring the national income from the projects to their accounts in the good name of contracts.

It takes imagination to see that savings bank wreckers, loan sharks, and investment swindlers, in their ambitions to grab the nation's wealth, take Africans' lives or reduce them to sub-human living. It takes imagination to see that the business of corrupt voters, fixed juries, seduced lawmakers, and debauched public servants in Africa. It is an impossible mission for anyone watching it through the eyes of the law and seeing how the nations are duped with law officers or agents carrying out the business. Africans have found themselves in the hands of such leadership that they now see themselves as passing through an organic phase and the thickening perils that block their path to progress or even existence.

Security to control African leadership is impossible because it is in the hands of the leadership. They, too, have turned it into the instrument of exploitation. Security in Africa cannot be trusted any more to be working for the national interests. It is accountable to the underworld.

Blind, instinctive reactions are no longer to be trusted. Social defense is now a matter for the experts—the rising of dikes against faithlessness and fraudulent calls for intelligent social attention. But the African public has not become shrewder in the grading and grilling of sinners. The African public cannot become shrewder simply because the defense of the nation rests in the hands of these mindless underworld sects, whose missions are to exploit the nations against the welfare of Africans.

What is wrong in African leadership is the moral insensibility. The directors who speculate in the security of the nation's corporations, the bankers who lend African depositors' money to themselves, the contractors who secretly rebate for their private graft, the builders who hire the walking delegates to harass their rivals with causeless strikes, the labor leaders who instigate strikes in order to be paid for calling it off, the publishers who bribe for the use of their published books as textbooks in the schools—these reveal in their faces nothing of wolf or vulture. Nature has not only foredoom leadership to evil by a double list of cruelty maker, greed, and jealousy it has equally castrated with their insensibility. African leadership are degenerates tormented by monstrous cravings. They want nothing more than what all Africans want–money, power, a good life–but they are in a hurry, and they are not particular as to the means on how they acquire the good life.

The nations' leadership prefers to prey on the anonymous public. They are equally not touchy on the individual African victims. They exploit the school child, the sick, the aged, and the helpless. They even exploit and prostitute their children. African leaders are horrible.

The nations' leadership has their connection between them and the touch of those who slip voters at the polls, the gangs who break other African heads with clubs and stones at the commands of the corrupt bosses. The leadership is able to keep them happy and gay with cheap drinks and loose sex. Thus they become consumers of custom made enemies, clients of criminals, offense agents of criminals, by requiring their subordinated to break the law. They have responsible agents also as valves to check the return flow of the proceeds and take note of the public reactions and the ringleaders to the reaction. Such ringleaders are hand picked, dealt with, or seduced to their illicit lives.

The leadership educates them on how to operate the criminal world and insist on results and tells them they are not interested in the method they use to get the results. The leadership method is fascinating, cruel, unethical, and detrimental to both the security and the progress of the countries. The leadership does not bribe, but employs and finances those who will bribe them. They do not lie, but make reporters admit that their articles on them are lies. They do not commit perjury, but hire men who foreswear against themselves. They do not cheat, but will hire embezzlers. They do not engage in robbery themselves, but engage the accountant who rebates the shipments. They do not physically shed the innocent blood, but bribe spectators to overlook and neglect installations of safety appliances that may result in losing several innocent lives. They are the buyers of criminals instead of they themselves participating in crime. The unpleasant details of the crimes are left to their hired hands. African leadership is social. Their smiles are broadest to local girls–students, nurses, teachers and secretaries. They know the best hotels in town, and in fact in the countries. They know the best drinks and the tastiest mixes. They even know the latest dancing steps and body movements. Age has nothing to do with their social lives.

The nation is the zone of these adulterers, rebaters, fraud promoters, monopolists, corrupt legislators, corporation-owned judges, bought bank examiners, etc. The leadership stays far away out of the scene and only operates their hired agents through a remote control.

They are perhaps good in their villages, may perhaps be the first to pay off their debts, stand up for friends, and may even be public spirited. They are ready to rescue babies in trouble, protect the weak, and help the poor widows. They are unevenly moral, but mindless in commercial and civic ethics. They may preach against giving and taking bribes and will not practice them, yet they employ men to do the dirty work for them.

Africans suffer from the results of these mindless actions. The leadership are equally Africans. There is only one prime goal in living, and that is to be happy. But African society has developed this into a dual purpose for living which now calls for merchandise in love and happiness.

The society has made Africans believe their selection of the best things in life, love and happiness are the creation of man, but these things are nature's gifts, as water and air are free.

There is not more freedom in Africa. Africans are now cut in the traffic of man-made inflation. Money can now buy happiness and love. It depends, of course, on what makes one happy. Happiness for the African can now be found in having cars, machines (motorcycles), holidaying abroad, owning houses, wives, and a bevy of concubines.

You are unhappy when you do not have the money to lavish on these luxuries; and without all these, love and happiness in Africa will ever continue to elude you.

The difference between Africans and their leadership is that the leadership can purchase, control, and exploit happiness and love. They can create them, own them, market them, inflate their prices, and monopolize them.

The leadership understands the working of the African mind. They understand the tribal order as against the civil order. By constantly stirring up on their behalf some sort of clannishness, local sectional partisans, etc., they kindle dying jealousies and check the rise to the civic spirit. It is in line with this clannishness that they want Africans to act together on a personal basis. They do not know what it is to rally on a principle, and they do not have principles. Participants in this clannishness are friends—in fact, brothers.

The nations' leadership understands sympathy and apathy as springs of conduct, but justice strikes them as hardly human. They see the law as a club to rescue their friends from and to smite their enemies with, but it has no claim of its own. They expect the victims to come back at them if they can, but they cannot see why everything may not be negotiated—settled out of court. The smart lawyers who understand their profession and remain dogmatic to the rule of law impress the leadership as fanatics and unearthly, as monsters who find their pleasure in making trouble for others. To the leadership, African society is only a matter of fighting out one's ways.

The leadership has no conscience. Their interest is self-centered, based on the jungle law of "survival of the fittest." Since they believe themselves as the fittest in the African society, they should be the lord of the African social and economic jungle.

They convert their illicit actions into righteous actions. The clan now sees the bribes as retaining fees, a license as a courtesy, inquiries as "scandal mongering," the investigator as a "nosy busybody," a protest as noise making or trouble making. Critics are "slanderers," public opinion is "unreasoning clamor," regulation is meddling.

The leadership agents are encouraged to see themselves as conforming to the norms of the society—in Rome do as Romans do—as asserting themselves in the higher law which greater enterprises have the right to command.

African leadership destroys the conscience of Africans by silencing the alert individuals who attempt to draw the attention of the masses or law to the evil actions of the leadership. They intimidate the news media by instructing them to confine themselves to the news, the preacher only to the gospel, the politician to party issues, the judge to his precedents, the teacher to his textbooks, the writer to his subjects—such are the methods of the leadership. But let them have the lessons from these scholars: African leadership will be sacrificed to the gods of justice, fairness, and righteousness.

Africa is perishing, and perishing fast, as a people in the hands of these avaricious leadership. Africans find themselves armed with blunt machetes or guns with blank cartridges in the midst of an ever-growling circle of wolves. There is no regulating system in the countries, and the nations are in the state of anarchy. Africans have lost their conscience. They have turned religion into sects, so they have no fear for the gods. They say that the gospel ideals are unscientific. As for the law, they say that they are alien to us. "They are colonial things."

Africans are therefore completely ill-equipped to combat the corruptions that prey on their society. It is a matter of time before the nations perish. This is, of course, a lame excuse for the African masses. As I tried to emphasize in the earlier chapter, the conventional Africans are all corrupt.

Their apathy to the misdeeds of their leadership encourages the wrong doers of the modern African leadership. If African societies were already divided into two classes as I tried to show in this chapter, the leadership class and the masses, each with its standards and opinions, then the masses would have been able to deliver effective corrective criticism that would have checked the leadership or would have been able to show the anger toward their leadership's actions.

But the leadership are European and US American-made Africans, hand picked from the streets and slums of the nations' cities. Their sense of superiority is not at all a short and feeble thing that wilts. They see themselves as gods and carry themselves thus at the back of their cars with underpaid drivers chauffeuring them. They are arrogant and ruthless about how they use their power.

The African masses envy such possessions and use of power, so they turn the other way at the misdeeds of their leaders, only hoping for the day they will be in the same position to exploit their nations.

They can therefore easily forgive the enemies of their society. Such an attitude is evil, for it shows the idea of supporting the wrong actions against the right. Africans have laid themselves down and asked the leadership to trample on them and with "Thanks, please."

Africans have joined their leaders in their misdeeds by turning the other cheek. They have indulged themselves in this habit of spoiling their leaders by condoning their crimes to the nations. They are quick to correct the wife-beater, and not the swindler of the national revenue, or the contractor who neglects his job after receiving some advance from the government, or the public servant who "sits" on files.

African leaders are then given a "pat on the back" while African masses snap at each other, grumbling at the inconvenience that such misdeeds of their leaders are causing them. Africans, out of apathy and fear, have led their countries into becoming an organic society in which the welfare of the nations are at the mercy of they themselves. The main task at present is getting Africans together to build societies which can boast of and maintain nations with reputable moral standards, statues, and the ability to check the onslaught of internal enemies.

Africans live on false principles, leaving both vices and crimes to take care of themselves. Both vices and crimes are detrimental to the nations' survival. Vice means a practice that harms on oneself, while crimes are rampant in the nations. They grow out of the relations Africans enter, hence the leaders of the nations find an opened door to walk in for their wrongdoings. They are called new forms of crimes against the nations.

The development of crimes in Africa has actually invited these leaders and their crude means to write laws for the nations. Let us glance through the membership Constituent Assembly in Nigeria. We can understand the personalities of the Nigerians who wrote the new Nigerian constitution. It was a noble idea for the late great Murtala Muhammed to commission the idea of producing a meaningful constitution for the nation. Out of enthusiasm I sent the late head of state this letter quoted below and copies of the letter were sent to over one thousand Nigerian politicians, natural leaders, university chancellors, and other Nigerians. Even the copy sent to the natural leaders in my home town was not made known to the people concerned, and Nigerian clannish bureaucracy must have prevented such an important document that affects the welfare of the nation from getting to the late Head of State Murtala Muhammed:

> This is the first time in the history of mankind that such quality of best minds in the nation has been selected to design a constitution that will guide the destiny of the nation's citizens. Such opportunity has never before occurred to any group of human beings–it is to say that such a thing happens once in a blue moon.

> Sir, this is my third reason for writing you this letter; you owe it to yourself as a Nigerian, to the history of your administration as a print

on the sands of time. You owe it to me and many other Nigerians to inject and emphasize the injection of the importance of our cultural heritage in the genes of our conceiving constitution, with the hope that the conception will bear for us a healthy constitution that will provide, direct, and preserve our destiny without strain.

Sir, it is my hope for Nigerians that the constitution will preserve our cultural heritage because it is this heritage that is responsible for what we are.

I am aware of the sentiments we have been led to develop on "tribes" or "tribalism." Sir, it is my dream and hope that, as those best minds sweat in their search for the best way to create this constitution, that they will remember Echezonam, Murtala, Okala, Ekon, Oviasuyi, Taiwo, etc., have different tribal cultures and bear in mind that this pluralism in our nation is an advantage, and not a disadvantage. For these, our "tribes" are something to be proud of, and not ashamed of. These tribes and their cultures can provide us numerous avenues to perceive our needs and problems, and solutions to them. It is a privilege that is rare among nations of the world. I must point out that Echezonam is first an Aniocha, then a Nigerian, then an African, then a citizen of the world. So, too, Oviasuyi is first a Bini, Ekon an Efik, Taiwo a Yoruba, Okala an Ijaw…. This is a fact that you and I know, Sir. I appeal to you to use your divine office to see that these tribal cultures are not snubbed by this, our new constitution, for they are responsible for our identities. Our so-called tribal cultures are responsible for our behaviors, which in fact control our thoughts with regard to life and death. Any constitution that disregards this fact, leaves the impression that such constitution is imposed upon the people; Sir, this is the surest way to exterminate the people—and clean them off the face of the earth. Sir, I cannot say that this earth has been good to me, but I think I love being here with my people as we carve our history on its face. Sir, I am appealing to you to use your offices to see that this, our constitution, represents the fact that Ekon is proud to be an Efik, and at the same time recognizes that Echezonam is equally proud to be an Aniocha as they shoulder a team with a task of building a Nigeria that will provide, guide, and protect our destiny. A destiny which occupies the same political territory known as Nigeria.

Sir, I recognize that this is a difficult task, but not an impossible one. I am very much aware that your problems with regard to this task is not an enviable one, for our tribal problems are not simple. Still, it is the duty of the government, your government, to keep reminding this panel of our nation's best minds, to portray a degree of responsibility to this, our pluralistic, tribalistic problem; mainly making sure that as they try weaving out a constitution that will protect our cultural heritage, our divine inheritance, the identity of our very persons, and the storehouse of our survival kit, they keep this uppermost in their minds.

Sir, I lay at your feet the future and destiny of every Nigerian, and Nigeria weighs heavily on the Articles, Sections, and clauses of this new constitution. It is the duty of governments–every government, in this case your government–to determine whether peace will prevail within Nigeria or another bloodshed. Sir, you have demonstrated where you stand in these few months of your administration, and many of us are very appreciative of that. Sir, it is your obligation to us as Nigerians, to provide us with the many things that will make life easier and more enjoyable; among these things the survival of every Nigerian ought to be, and is prime in your administrative decisions, and hopefully that the same thing goes for this new constitution. The key to this survival is our divine cultural heritage, for our cultures even though they are multiple, are responsible for what we are. If the new constitution overlooks this fact, it is committing genocide to Nigerians. If Nigerians fail to recognize this fact and thereby fail to demand the protection of our "tribal" cultures, I must point out that the end will be mass suicide for Nigerians. Let us not hope for that.

I am sending copies of this letter to as many of our traditional cultural elites as my small income can provide mailing, and to as many as I can locate their addresses. Sir, you have done what is expected of your leadership, and I am arrogantly proud of that. The rest is left for Nigerians. For this reason, I am sending copies of this letter to our cultural elites, for as I address every sentence in this letter to you, I am also addressing the sentences to them, and to every Nigerian.

It is your duty to see that the constitution represents the interest of Nigerian subjects. Our cultural elite owe it to us as the people they rule and represent to point out their individual interests and concern as "tribal" groups to the fifty-man panel that will weave out this, our constitution. I am demonstrating to them with this letter that this is their only chance to inject their concern and the interest of the people into the constitution.

It is a pity that the old constitution robbed them of this right. It instead removed their divine rights, cultural rights, and gave them to the colonialists, who mortgaged them to irresponsible Nigerians on the basis of the highest bidder. Sir, this bred and is still breeding for us elite who only know their rights, but are working overtime stealing other people's rights, and hiding them from their duties. The old constitution destroyed our religious heritage, thereby seduced and corrupted our morals. It is shameful to think of Nigerians now as people without conscience. In fact, it is lamentable to think of this. This is the problem that you are facing in corruption in high places and among our business elites. It is the old constitution that failed to provide us with an adequate educational system. Instead, they gave us a system that looked down on our culture, seduced our youths and raped their morals. It is the old constitution that is responsible for the educational system that destroyed creativity among our youths so much that today millions of Nigerians go to bed hungry every night while the country has been producing specialists with diplomas and university degrees for over thirty years. Heaven knows the population of Nigerians with diplomas and university degrees in economics and various branches of business–and yet the country's economics is a mess! No Nigerian brain could have borne the thought of what would have become of us if Nature had not blessed us with unexpected wealth. Still, it is shamefully annoying that Nigeria produces millions of barrels of oil every day–and Nigerian cars are stranded in the streets for lack of oil to move them. It is shameful to watch Nigerians with outstanding degrees and diplomas in business prostituting themselves among foreign businessmen who are far less qualified for commissions on connections they hope to make for themselves with regard to obtaining government contracts for them. It is sad, very sad, to know that Nigeria has been able to produce millions of graduates from secondary schools to doctors of philosophy in different fields of human needs for survival–and these graduates can only be teachers. Those who are teachers got into the profession to perpetuate the norms of the old constitution. Those who got into government are unable to create new avenues to expand government revenues or to generate initiatives to exploit the existing avenues in the government to increase government revenues, which, in turn, will affect their incomes and their standard of living. Instead, they resort to corruption, bribery, misappropriation of funds, and awarding of contracts only to those who can deposit their commissions in foreign banks, of which the Swiss banks are notorious. Sir, it is the old constitution which is responsible for all this–not Nigerians. Is it not suicidal that our youths are ashamed of their towns and villages? Most of us are ashamed to speak our mother tongue, and do not like living in the land that nursed our birth. This is, in fact, leading eventually to not liking, or appreciating ourselves and ours. Sir, is this not committing suicide? It is the old constitution that is responsible for this.

Let us hope that this our new constitution, will not encourage the norms of the old constitution but find ways to eliminate them and influence of the old constitution.

And so Nigerians went ahead and got themselves an alien constitution in their effort to Americanize themselves. Americans can readily testify their constitution has truly produced laws which perpetuated and protected crimes in their country.

Laws are calculated apparatus designed for controlling the society, but where it falls into the hands of such elite as African leaders, it becomes a tool for exploiting the society.

It is funny, though, that countries in Africa have always been ruled by alien laws right from the colonial days to the independent Africa. Imported laws designed for enslaving a people can never work for the interest of the enslaved people. It is this law that African leaders seized and applied on their nations in their exploiting their nations.

The law legalized stealing in different sophisticated forms. It is now in Africa as a disease is in the body. It encounters obstacles in the nation's natural processes. Its clash with such natural processes, if not well braced, means death for the nations in a very near future. The nature of leadership and crime in Africa denies Africans their self-respect and their human dignity. It shocks and later seduces the righteous. It disheartens and demoralizes the weak and the young. It destroys the nations since Africans cannot check crimes within their borders and therefore are prepared to perish.

The law's main obligation in Africa today is on the side of the sophisticated criminals, and Africans' apathy summons the society to draft more of its force to aid the criminals to achieve their goals. The leadership can now do what they like in Africa and have so developed wings they are able to gag the critics, hobble the investigators, intimidate the judges, hood-wink the press, and muzzle the law. They are now drunk with power in their offices, clubs, churches, schools, legislatures, and courts. They boldly make their stand and ruin the innocent, shredding the reputation of the righteous, destroying the career and opportunities of the rivals, dragging down scholars and pastors, the editors of the press, and businessmen in the mud. African leaders are mindless and horrible. They have corrupted and destroyed the soul of the nations, and stand with fists ready, fingers on the triggers, clubs raised, tongues wagging, all in readiness to fight the opposition or any African who dares to raise the eyebrows.

Has African been progressive since the departure of the cutthroat colonialist? One can easily assert that the answer to this question must be matter of opinion. On the other hand, it is a fact these European imperialists left Africa with only a few "junior colleges," arms of the European universities which are now the full-grown universities. Now, the same Africans may be boasting of having near one hundred universities, several other institutions of higher learning.

African economic products were marketed by these European gangsters in their countries' markets, while Africans only waited for a handout of the products of their land and sweat. And the same Africans are able to nationalize the same European property in their countries, and in some occasions order the European residents to pack and leave within a given time. Well, progressive has to be redefined by the dictionary composers if all these do not mean that Africa has been progressive.

Then look at Africans. There are millions of them with university degrees. They run their schools and civil service. They even write and produce their constitution. Their children are numerous and robust and healthy. Africans walk like giants across the world claiming to be seeking for or making peace. Well, one cannot be wrong to assert that Africa has been progressive.

Yes, Africa has been progressive. But the civil servants in the hands of Africans have been mindlessly insensitive to the needs of the Africans. They have made themselves masters of the people they are supposed to be serving. They are now experts in giving contracts, only with the hope of remodeling the same job a year later, still on contract.

The ferocity of leadership, the friction of the corruption in the natural process of life, the stench of the philosophies, confuse Africans so that the sense of right and wrong eludes them. Never in the history of the countries have Africans been so exploited, civil servants so mindless, girls so loose, youths so irresponsible, workers so unconcerned, Africans so poisoned with synthetic foods, concerned Africans so harassed, investors so fleeced, and the honest so tempted and seduced. Leadership in Africa, and their kind– the "silent majority"–as the stockholders, the legislature, and the councilors are alike. This "silent majority" does not only know what is going on, but so long as they are comfortable, they resent having inconvenient knowledge thrust upon them. A reverend once told me that Nigeria is all right as long as no one would kick a sleeping dog. So the "silent majority" lets the sleeping dog lie. But Nigeria's problem is not a sleeping dog. It is a fully charged bomb waiting for naked fire to set it into explosion.

African leadership is mindless. They look after their kind. They are raped by tribal, religious, or secret society antipathy, prejudice, or caste pride. They are known by their political ambitions and social aspirations without being qualified for them. They exact personal subservience and indulge themselves in petty tyranny. Never offend them, for they are known for holding grudges and will never rest until they teach their rivals or enemies a lesson. Their ambition is to ruin their enemies and rivals out of malice, simply because they stand in their way. African leadership is dreadfully insensitive to the needs and feelings of the Africans as nations. They do not feel the restraints that conscience and public sentiments lay on them. They fear no law, and public sentiments lay on them. They fear no law or public indignation far less than any simple-minded, honest African. They have cowed Africans into numbness so that Africans have fallen into the group of the "silent majority." They cannot loathe their leadership, they are even through their eye service—"yes sir," "ejo sir," "diokpa, doma sir," etc.—to pick some of the crumbs from the leadership and condone and approve their illicit actions. Far from it, they cannot disapprove their actions by speaking out their mind or ostracizing the leadership. They cannot convert the leadership or animate them with patriotic spirit or love for social service. These have little or no effect on the leadership, if Africans tried any of them, or on the tenor of their self-appointed positions, or on the corporations they have imposed on Africans. The leadership is an entity that transmits their greed, not their conscience, and expects profit, but not unpopularity.

They alienate themselves from their hired criminal hands. Each year finds a greater distance between them and their corruption dragnets. Each year increases their number and sees them more scattered and more powerful. Each year sees the leadership's exploitative establishment and the millions of Africans who furnish the money, thereby making it harder for their conscience to be reached and humanized. The leadership practice of watering the Africans and unloading the infusion upon African public is marvelously potent in banishing humanity and decency from the leadership and their hired criminals who do their dirty jobs for them. The leadership has so infused their illicit activities, or exploitative activities among Africans that to doubt the activities is to doubt the national conscience, and the individual Africans themselves.

The leadership finds ways to convert the honest Africans through capitalizing and marketing the last turn of their business. This has a diabolic power to convert and seduce the honest who have exchanged their lives' savings, purchasing shares in the Dracula's fangs they call the business establishments the leaders created as a gateway into the heart of the African economy. This is what they call investment into developing Africa, and the way responsible honest Africans sell their souls to the monstrous cankerworms eating down the fabrics—the cornerstone of the countries.

Development projects therefore have to look for such hardcore mindless society exploiters who can drive able Africans like cattle and reluctant Africans to comply. With their remoteness and anonymity, African leaders develop their property and "prosper" through proposed prosperity of Africa at the nations' expense, while the respect for local sentiment, the rights of other, and the law of the land are trampled under their giant and hurried strides to grab the money.

Africans take all these in silence without standing up against them. They do not will for the potholes on their roads, the smelling gutters around their homes, the hospitals without drugs, the mindless civil servants, the stagnant traffic lines, the undisciplined youths, etc., but they have them. Africans seem to demand such only because they fail to realize what they are doing when they exert their last penny encouraging their leaders. However harmless their intentions, their greed for the money throws the countries into the hands of domineering, arrogant, unscrupulous, mindless leaders. The leaders have only one ambition, and that is to obey the demands of their corrupt sects.

Africans as a matter of fact are not all lawbreakers, unpatriotic, or hardhearted. Many Africans are peace-loving, or at least there are many wishing and trying to be patriotic to their countries and fellow men; but whatever qualities these Africans possess, they are suppressed under the whims of their nation's leadership who control their property and gradually seduced them into the social sin that menaces the nations.

Seeking for the Social Identification

It is in the nature of animate beings to be assertive. This assertion they present among themselves and divide their activities which they apportion among themselves. It is through this apportionment of roles that these organic beings assert their personalities.

Read the above paragraph again and observe that I said in the first sentence that *it is in the nature of animate beings*–organic beings–*to be assertive.* Plants, insects, reptiles, and anything with life and form (body) are animate and organic. Such a being is designed by nature to be assertive, not out of its own choice. The assertion is an imposition by nature and the beings have to obey this dictation from nature or cease to exist.

But how do they assert themselves? It is not possible to review how these beings assert themselves one by one. Rather, I would like to pick only a plant and an animal to illustrate this.

Let us define *assertion* first. Assertion with regards to this book is an insistence of the being to be noticed or recognized, an imposition of one's image on others; attempts of a being to usurp other beings' rights; an unlawful attempt to steal other beings' chances to be noticed; Attempts by a being to deny other beings their rights by forcing them out of existence–out of notice. The definition of this simple word, assertion, is so extent that it may be as endless as life itself, for it is with assertion the life maintains its existence, hence we assert, self-identification is ability–fitness for a being to suppress other beings to project oneself or need against the interest of others; which is existence–is survival of the fittest beings.

Let us take a plant. How does it assert itself? The assertion of a being must involve other beings. But for the assertion to be meaningful, the assertion must be with the being noticeable with other beings of the same kind, though the assertion goes on with the imposition of a being on the universe, with the attempt to dominate it.

Assertion has to start with life. So assertion starts with a kind of plant, and its struggle to come out of the seeds. It is in this tender age of the plant that nature exposes itself as mysterious, wonderful, and wicked. The mystery is the formation of a different kind of life from the seeds. The wonder is how this tender life is able to break the coat of the seed or the shell in case of kernels and still find its way through the soil to join all other living beings in the world. This journey is both mysterious and wonderful. The struggle requires a degree of guided intelligence for the helpless baby plant.

It is during this struggle to reach the world of other beings that the assertion of self begins. Where the seeds are planted together in a whole or are crowded in a space, the assertion is vivid. Some of the young plants may die in the struggle, others may weaken, while the able ones blossom. Even the dead plants or the weak ones finally form food for the able ones.

This is the result of assertion at that tender age. Then comes the adolescent age. One observes that not all the plants grow alike. Some become dwarfs; some grow tall, but look pale; others who could assert themselves better grow huge, bustling with health. The dwarf and the tall pale plants are treated as weeds and are weeded out to allow the healthy plants better space to grow. Again, it is easy to notice the reason behind the plants asserting themselves. It is the struggle for existence, and that gives rise to what we know as the jungle law—survival of the fittest. Some of the seeds and plants which fall back at the struggles are or may first not be healthy seeds when planted; but even where sick seeds were planted with adequate advantages, nature is so generous it will so aid the young plant to assert itself in its earthly environment so the young plant will sail through the struggles to survive. At the same time a healthy seed planted with poor advantage will produce sick young plants; and a healthy young plant in a hostile environment will perish on the wayside or make it through as an invalid without reproducing, and when it does it will be a poor specimen.

The same thing happens in the animal kingdom. A visit with keen observation to a farm duplicates the same pattern of the struggles for survival, only the brutality is more vivid. The beings, such as the chickens, are seen eating the weak ones alive. The lizards are seen swallowing the younger ones alive. The understanding of the survival of the fittest is very clear in the animal kingdom.

Only the insect world is smarter than the rest of the beings in the universe. No wonder King Solomon advised in the Christian guidebook, the Bible, " . . . fools go to the ants and be wise." The insects—the bees, white ants, etc.—are the only beings which understand the need for co-existence, an existence that employs the weak with its poor advantages and the strong with its inherited advantages for the good of the group.

There are of course animals of the wild which exercise the same intelligence as the insects. Such animals are those that move in groups: the elephant, lion, and monkey. Still, the weak are trampled when the herd, pride, or family are in a rush. Watch them eating. It is survival of the fittest, only that rawness of nature of the strong feeding straight on the weak is not glaring, but it is there.

Even with such intelligence in the animal kingdom there is slavery—the underprivileged, the weak serving the privileged and the strong. Though this is termed slavery, the weak that gives the service is given protection, and what is termed service may be training for the young ones being initiated into the culture of the group.

Watch a pride of lions. The male, the king of the jungle, sleeps for about eighteen hours or more. The female does the hunting and waits for the king to eat first. While eating, the senseless young ones dare not get near him. Even after eating, when resting, any other lion dare nor disturb him. But in case another big male lion or other danger invades the pride, the male lion does the fighting alone, and when it fails to protect the pride, it voluntarily leaves while another male lion takes its place. So, one can safely point out the same sense of watching a family of monkeys or a herd of elephants, the pattern is almost the same as that of a pride of lions.

The study of the family of *Homo sapiens*, the "wise guys"—man—is fairly in the same pattern, only that the exploitation of the underprivileged without offering them adequate protection back is more profound. This is what it has been since man started living in families. But it was not all that bad, simply because what was termed exploitation was regarded as a way of growth, since a slave served a term only to be free to marry his master's daughter or to become his master's partner or rival. This kind of exploitation is voluntary on the side of the underprivileged or, in some cases, imposed on the war victims of criminals.

This kind of exploitation is primitive and outdated with modern man. Exploitation of man must be based on making him realize he is being exploited because of his inferior advantage to the one exploiting him. He is to be exploited without protection and until he dies. Even if the dead body can be put in use, that should be done without showing any feelings. The underprivileged are not regarded as human beings. They are inferior species of human beings who are only in slavery—and Hitler's Germans and the Jews confirm this. It is interesting, though, to note that in either case of the history of slavery or in the case of German Jews in the days of Hitler, exploitation "was always for the good of the exploiting nations and never for a group being exploited." European and African slave dealers, or "slavers," went into the human merchandise for the good of their respective countries, and slavery built the "New World"—America—of today. The same slavery created the European industrial revolution, the cornerstone of European economic development. An English author and economist, commenting on the evil effect of slavery, put it: "…slavery is bad, but it is less bad for the enslaving nations"– meaning it was good for the enslaving nations. Where they enslaved themselves, they used the exploitation for the overall development of the nation; hence the English slaves were sent to the Americas and Australia to develop the farms and plantations and were later used to colonize the lands.

This is the modern exploitation of man on his own species. This is the scientific era where exploitation is extended to using the man with a remote control to exploit himself for the good of the other. The Ghanaian President Kwame Nkruma and other politicians of his time call this type of exploitation of nations neo-colonialism.

Exploitation is a natural phenomena based on self-identification, which is consciously or unconsciously exposed by an individual in its attempt to the necessities of survival. The self asserts itself and imposes its demand on others. This imposition can be diplomatic or forceful.

The fact is that survival is vital to self. It either projects (asserts or identifies) itself or perishes. This behavior is universal to all organism-animate beings. The attainment of this projection, assertion, or identification depends on the quality of the inner drive of the self. This self involves itself in this adventure for survival's sake on how it perceives itself, thinks of itself, values itself, and the various actions it takes to enhance and defend itself.

It may be difficult to notice these moves taken by beings to identify themselves in their environments in their attempts to impose their demands on other beings with a positive ambition to satisfy their needs first, not minding how the others survive in the same environment.

This organism's ability is to secure its wants in the environment by projecting itself so positively that it suppresses others until it satiates itself, even at the disadvantages of other beings in the environment. This intention is not achieved in the first attempt. The achievement is controlled in persistent attempts which build experience. And with this experience the survival of the being is guaranteed, while the fate of other beings are subjected to serving the needs of the experienced being in the environment.

The assessment of the being of subjecting itself to exploit other beings is also controlled by the value of the projected self attached to the value of the object to be extracted from environment.

The organism's measurement of the value of the required object in the environment and its experience to exploit it provides it with the self-assessment of its ability to impose itself on others in making its claims over the necessity. Its knowledge about its ability, if this ability has attended the point of imposing itself on others at will, puts the organism in the self-actualized state along the line of what may be termed heredity. The being becomes more differentiated, more expanded, more autonomous, and more luxuriant. It becomes the monarch of the kingdom.

This is noticed when the being is observed over a long period of time. There is always a forward movement to assert or identify itself. It is this ongoing tendency which is the only force that keeps the being in constant shape in its deadly mission against others.

This self-actualization is accomplished with persistent struggles and pain. The being engages itself in the struggle and stands the pain because of the creative urge of growth—the outcome of survival. The child learns to walk in spite of its initial trouble. He learns to ride a bike under the same strain. The adult learns to dance in spite of his awkwardness and embarrassment.

The being goes through all these struggles to assert itself in the environment, and as a result of interaction with others and the environment and constant self-evaluation, its structure is formed as a consistent conceptual pattern of perception of characteristics and relationship of the identified self and its value and interests in the environment.

The being then becomes aware of other things which enable it to distinguish itself as an able object in the environment. When it has learned this distinction, it then perceives something belongs to it, while other things belong to the environment, and those that belong to it are those it needs. All these help it to assess itself and its values in the environment.

Life (living) is a struggle, and it involves all beings from the microorganism to the *Homo sapien*. All is based on the need to survive. In survival the strong and the privileged must prey on the weak, the disadvantaged, and the underprivileged to survive. That is why life is brutal and nature is heartless. It is the moral attachment to the activities that bred such adjectives. Afterwards life is to be lived, whether it is brutal and nature heartless. It is difficult for man to notice life and nature with these patterns when he cuts the vegetable leaves or fruits belonging to another being, picks some flowers, or kills the cows or chickens. These are lives belonging to other beings. Rather than see the brutality of his actions against other beings he designs a philosophy which provides an umbrella under which he hides with the excuse that he had dominion over them. The same rationalization gives a lion, a tiger, a boar, a dominion over man, or man over man.

The analysis I have gone through above in this chapter on self-identification is to show the reader man is not an exception in the game beings play for survival. But man is not like other beings, so he asserts; he is a rational animal and therefore applies reason in his actions. He recognizes the need for corporate life and advocates it, yet life is dogmatic, and the unprivileged, the weak, are saddled with the ugly fate of being subjected to the wolves who are in the forms of human beings as their neighbors. The nakedness of the gruesome affair and the like is always a new creation of wickedness, which appear in the forms of secret and deadly methods such as prison, ambush, witchcraft, even naked future in an exhibition of one's lordship of the other. As the other suffers the pain, the one who inflicts the pain fiddles in jubilation of the misfortune he has or is causing on his neighbor. This is man all right, the rational being who finds glory in destroying his kind.

We must not forget that the title of this chapter is "Seeking for the Social Identification." Following the analysis above on identity which is broken down to self-projection or self-assertion; it is therefore easy to know why it is that seeking for identity is vital.

The Europeans came to Africa and imposed their identity on the Africans whose culture readily gave in to the Europeans assertions. The Europeans did not waste time imposing themselves on the stage of neo-colonialism.

They (the Europeans) employed all the forms of exploitations to exploit the Africans, not minding the effect on them, and Africans submitted in silence until they realized they were perishing fast under such mindless exploitations. We will talk more of this in the next chapter, "Loss of Cultural Heritage: Colonialism."

Africans of old, those who were alive years before colonialism, recognized the mindlessness that follows the seeking society and did not only eliminate it but looked down on it. The Attainment to Humanity. The society they created discouraged it. They found ways to destroy emphasis on "I" and "me," and imposed on Africans the importance of "we" and "us." They exploited themselves for the good of themselves. Attempts of selfishness were destroyed and ostracized. The affairs of the group (clan) were run by the group and individuals, even the sick and the aged were provided for.

The images (personalities) of the individuals were measured through the ancestral father of the clan and not the individuals' achievements. The individuals' struggles were to maintain the ancestral pride; in fact there is a saying among Enuani people stating that "A child has a cock, but it crows in front of a man's (his father's) house."

It is not so today. The European has destroyed this godly set-up that humanized Africans. They imposed on Africans the mindlessness of individualism, the brutality of capitalism, the lies in diplomacy, the deceits of politicalisms, and the cunning of constitutions.

The Europeans exploited Africans under the law. The law was approved by their constitution, which was based on their political isms. Africans, in their ambition to regain their lost social identity and thereby protect their economic resources which guarantee them survival on this earth's environment, rose against the Europeans, who bowed out, leaving their stooges in form of Africans to carry on the exploitation in forms of "neo-activities;" hence, Africans see their own brothers exploiting them even worse than the Europeans did.

Africans rule and exploit their countries now. Millions of Africans who do not belong to the leadership stay aside, wishing and hoping for the day the leadership will come to them, and those holding the reins of power stay firm on the saddle and make sure that the "reins of power" do not slip from their grips. One kind of drama in African society! The African masses struggling to get on the African social horse; the African leaders who are already on the horse are seen kicking off the African masses and with the social reins whipping them to exploit the nations for their maintenance.

What Africans do to get out from this their slavery chain of exploiting themselves for the underworld is what I call "social identification." They have to identify themselves to the Africans on the nations' social horses. The identification must be glaring to convince those with the "reins of power" that they belong to the same sect, tribe, church, or the Africans who lack this social identity become the "baboons that work for the monkey to chop."

I loathfully watched the sad feelings that pretentiously existed among the Ibos against the Hausas in Northern Nigerians during the Nigerian-Biafran war. That was toward the end of the war. This Ibo man could speak Hausa very well. The feeling then was that for an Ibo to survive in Nigeria, he must be an Hausa man. And to be an Hausa, he must speak the language, skin-shave his hair—the malam style—and dress in their big jumper. I said I loathfully watched this Ibo man because I was very much aware the Ibos like him were those who used Biafran sufferings to collect money from sympathizers and used the money for their private needs.

African masses are worse than this Ibo man. This Ibo man could identify what was "Hausa" and then identify himself with it. The problem with the conventional African is he does not know what is African, so he identifies with what he sees. And unfortunately what he sees is corrupt Africans of individualism, capitalism, sectionalism, tribalism, nepotism, secret societies, loose sexual moral laxity, bribery, mindlessness, get-rich-fast not minding what they do to who they use to get rich, living above one's means, fraud in establishments, willfully doing the wrong thing and hoping to beg when caught, sitting on files for the services the civil servant is paid for, "pushing" to usurp other people's rights, thugs and underworld, pimping and prostitution, irresponsible parents and teachers who produce irresponsible youths, political "riggers," connectors and "pluggers"—the dealers. Think of any evil—that is what African is today. These are what Africans have to identify with to survive or they will be weeded out of the earthly garden as weeds.

It is pathetic to study Africans critically and come out with deductions as I have above on what is the modern Africa. Go through what is Africa again and look again at those contested elections to represent their fellow Africans in their various political houses. Both those who failed to be elected and the elected ones are the same. Pick them one by one and match them to what I pointed out above as what makes up the Africa of today.

Africans of today are hopeless, yet they are all Africans have to identify with. The aim of identification is to be like the object being identified to social identifications if horrible, and the future of Africa is at the mercy of the gods whose norms have been grossly violated.

The hope in Africa is hopeless, and that would have been education. Education has always been a corrective media for human societies throughout the history of mankind. But education in Africa is hopeless. It ruins the nation's intelligent youths and perpetuates the nation's ills. Africans, out of nationalism, set out to produce Chinua Achebe, Camara Laye, Gabriel Okara, Ngugi, Oyono, Ekwensi, Ayi Kwei Arma, Mmunonye, J. P. Clark, and a few others. These are the nation's creative writers, and Africa is proud of them. And that is enough reward for them. But how do African educators utilize these talents? In their ambition to Europeanize their marvelous creation, they overlook their messages on the causes of the nation's social ills or the vivid descriptions of the nation's social ills. For example, if African educators had given *No Longer at Ease* the attention it deserved in making (forcing—not through corporal punishments) one see the ills of living above one's means and seducing one, allowing himself to be seduced into social sins, the nations would have made good steps toward nation building through raising dependable youths. No, Achebe is not an Englishman. The writing is not Shakespearean. The author had written it to catapult himself into the elite class and entertain the academic class. It is sad, very sad indeed, that the ambitions of the nations' creative authors who labor to expose their countries' social ills are handled so lightly.

There are other African authors—the question and answer copywriter—the rubber stamp makers of model answers. They are those who perpetuate the ills in the country. They ruin the intellects of the nation's youths. They stifle the youths' creative abilities. They perpetuate the colonial mentality in the nations. They robotize the youths and kill their curiosity. They remove the humanity in the youth and monsterize them.

These rubber stamp authors of model answers and questions in all subjects do not know the harm they are doing to the nations. They have a quick easy way to make fast money and have seized the chance.

The examination bodies are the Alpha and Omega of the African academic world—the WABC, RSA, GCE—the nation's universities and institutes of higher learning, etc. It is annoyingly sad Africans set out to destroy themselves after running out the colonialists. They create the conditions of passing examinations by rote. Thus, they produce for the nations' tape recorders in the form of educated youths who can only work on routines at the nations' establishments or as businessmen and the middlemen calibers. Look around from high school to the nations' Ph.d.'s in both science and art subjects—how many of them are in self-initiative creative employment of their own? On average, I'll say practically none. And, in fact, I have seen none.

Their educationalists have produced parasites out of Africans who now function in the espionage into the nation's corruption world. These educationalists have produced for the nations mindless academicians who now parade themselves as errand boys—the dragnets of the corrupt world. These educationalists are Africans directing African destiny. They have created a society we know as conventional Africa and the people we know as Africans; these Africans are what is left for the social identity of the nations.

The future of Africa as a nation with such citizens to be identified with is sealed and hopelessly sealed into doom. Africans live on hope the hopelessness will be better. They have to, for Africans know they are watching this, their hope, continuously go hopeless, because the modern Africa is now producing Africans who kill their sons, Africans of alcoholic and drug addictions, Africans who call back their sons from abroad to exploit them until they die of high blood pressure. Africans who know more than themselves and are allowed to criticize others, only criticizing aloud to assert themselves, not believing what they are saying. Africans who are sadists, who are only happy at causing misfortune to their neighbors and are thrilled at their misfortunes. Africans who are happy only when they assure themselves that they are cheating their neighbors or have cheated them. Africans who hate themselves and work overtime Europeanizing and Americanizing themselves, only to come out as counterfeit Americans and Europeans— Africans of "bin-to's" and pretended "bin-to's."

Loss of Cultural Heritage: Colonialism

Any red-blooded African who goes through the previous chapters in this book and knows, too, the chapters are factual on what Africans have been turned into will be so revolted by the ruthless colonial exploitations and political oppressions of Africans who have now turned Africans to eating themselves so mindlessly that doom appears to be the only prediction for the nations' future.

Colonialism has gone, and it has been years since it left Africa. Why blame the ills of the nations on the Europeans? Yes, they have gone, but they left their brainwashed Africans and their systems to carry on their bloody and mindless exploitations. Look at the nations' judiciary systems; visit any of the nations' courts; review the nations' education system; watch their lectures, examination, and graduation systems; look at their print and electronic media; and review the emphasis in their functions, then watch the African, even the youth born in the cities, and tell me that colonialism has left Africa.

Take a look at the African social elite—the nations' leaders; study their interests, their ambitions. Is their aim not on the exploitation of their less fortunate Africans for their (the elite) self-centered ends? Have they not made all the social ills in the countries legalized industries? Have they not led Africans to see them as virtues and not as vices, crimes, and sins to the nations? Colonialism—yes, colonialism—created African leaders and charged them with the duty of exploiting their fellow Africans and Africa. And the worst, colonialism armed the African leaders with the tool which they effectively use to disarm Africans who oppose them in their devilish murderous mission against their people. African leaders exert all their physical and mental energies in carrying out the assignment.

Take another look at African leaders and compare them with European colonialism. Was the colonialism at a proper screening not based on gross deception, hypocrisy, oppression, and exploitation? Are African leaders not maintaining these activities of the colonialists long after colonialism is said to have gone?

But what were the Africans before colonialism? How were the Africans to themselves? I met the last laps of colonialism and was not blessed with the practical experience of what Nigerians were before colonialism. I was born into the European glorified Nigerian slavery they called colonialism. But I like to see myself as a student of history and like to use it as a tool for reasoning.

One thing is a living fact, and very vital in this chapter, and may be in this book as a matter of fact. That is that there was nothing as both the word or physical patch or area of the earth that was called African. Colonialism created African countries as the property of the European countries based on the Berlin conference in 1885, which divided Africa for the European countries. So, it is very obvious African nations are nations borne out of the European exploitation of Africans, and Africa is the Europeans' attempts to disguise slavery they claimed they abolished, only to continue the slavery in the name of colonialism.

So, we had African nations–the Enuani, Ga, Wolof, Kikuyu, Zulu, etc.– become tribes within African nations. Still, these people became African nations not knowing their national identities had changed. They were Africans in the perceptions and mentality of Europeans. The Africans got to the classroom and began to study the European possessions in Africa, and the poor Africans first of all discovered they are French, German, Spanish, and British territories–the European countries' property, slaves just like the Indians, Mexicans, Burmese, etc. Then, under these classifications, they find themselves as the Nigerian, Kenyan, Ugandan, Togolese, Senegalese, etc.

The system of conditioning the African, which modern psychology calls brainwashing, did not explain to the young African scholar how he turned overnight to become Nigerian, Ghanaian, South African, etc. The brain-washing removed his local gods that controlled his behavior and replaced them with Christianity, the custodian of the alien god. He was forced to dis-own the gods of his people. The alien god championed that the treacheries, and exploitations of Jacob against the honesty of his brother Esau. It assert-ed and imposed individualism and capitalism on the African scholars who, in fact, had forgotten that nature had made them as an Enuani, Fanti, Kikuyu, Wolof, etc.

Enough of history. Our concern here is why are these Africans and what they were before these Arab and European exploiters, oppressors, suppres-sors of human rights to satisfy their self-centered goals changed. It is clear by now who the Africans were before they became what they are today. Now, what were they before the Arab and European colonization. They were the people who lived in trusteeship. They trusted themselves. They believed in themselves and had no fear for themselves.

The fragments of what they were lingered during the colonial days. The society was humane. People could leave their valuables without fear of them being stolen.

Every elder man in the community is a father to any younger person to him. He does not only answer the father. He lives up to the obligation, and rightly expects and in fact demands his rights from the younger person. So, too, is every elderly woman in the community. She, too, is the mother to any younger person to her and lives up to the motherhood.

The aged, the young, and even the stranger were the sons and daughters—the children of the gods of the land. These gods dictated the norms of the society, which in reality controlled the people's behaviors.

The priests to the gods were the custodians of the norms, and they mortgaged the dispenser of the justice to the elders. The priest, the elders, and the people were servants—honest servants of the gods and the people. Here ties the key to the trusteeship among them. The brotherhood among them was under the umbrella of their gods. Here, too, is the origin of partnership among them. They were ours among themselves in groups. They were partners to themselves, and they were their "brother's keepers." They were partners in troubles, in needs, and in fortune.

They were proud people, proud of their achievements, and proud of their very beings. They saw themselves as noble men, and associated their names and titles with the greatness, noble, and wonderful creations of the gods.

The people were free. They were free from fear. They were free to labor and enjoy the fruit of their labor. They had freedom of movement, freedom of association, and freedom of speech. They were free as nature intended them to be.

Upon all, these people were happy people who lived in healthy and rich environments. Their lands had healthy and fat animals and crops. It was a land where "milk and honey flowed." They lived in a land of feasting and the youth was happy and responsible.

These were what the Africans were when the colonialists came and imposed treacherous, hostile, evil forces in the people's way of life. Cultures are not negotiable. A negotiated culture is an adulterated culture. An adulterated culture is alien to the people, and therefore cannot fend for the interest and welfare of the people. The colonialists imposed this negotiated culture in the disguise of indirect rule on the Africans, under the strange creation of the nation-hoods Gold Coast, Nigeria, Kenya, Tanganyika, Tunisia, etc. Nigerians of course resisted (see Chinua Achebe's *Things Fall Apart*), but fell at last and since then have lost their totem (see the author's *The Lost Totem of the Cheerful Savage*).

So, Africans found themselves and their land as exploited people and territory by the Europeans to guarantee their property and territory—to guarantee their people in Europe a better standard of living. Africa therefore became a source of raw materials, cheap labor, and a dumping ground for surplus goods to be sold to them at very high prices. Thus, Africa became avenues for the colonists' capital investments only for the benefits of the Europeans, against the interests and welfare of Africans.

Africans were not, of course, fools. It did not take them time to imagine at least the intentions of these Europeans. The Europeans at the same time noticed the African's feelings and came up with their "do-gooders." Doctrines, the exploitation doctrine, described under their economic principle–capitalism, communism, socialism, individualism, etc.–the doctrine of partnership, sold to Africans through Christianity with the theory of "love thy neighbor as you love thyself"; and the doctrine of the "oneness" of humanity, and still expected the Africans to play the inferior role of the servants while they (the Europeans) remained the masters.

With all these doctrines, these Europeans believe in the theory of the survival of the fittest–that is the stronger people must exploit the weaker people for the good and welfare of the stronger people.

Africans surprisingly found themselves in a battlefield with the European wolves and their technological strength, armed with nothing but bare hands. The Europeans dominated the battle, and therefore called out the terms, that the economic deals will be again on their side at the expenses of Africa, and that exports from Africa to Europe must exceed imports to Africa, and furthermore that African economic exploitation must be at their own monopoly, not allowing Africans to deal with any other nation or nations. So Africa remained a colony which supplied them raw materials, a marketplace for the Europeans to sell their manufactured goods from Europe, and field for investment of their surplus capital.

Africa then became open without disguise or pretence. European's organized groups of people outside Europe in a foreign land, a settlement of Africans, a European state outside Europe, territorial units geographically separated from Europe–exploitation colonies of the Europeans.

Africans found themselves bearing the "white man's burden." The burden weighed heavy on their shoulders, and they rebelled. But the Europeans were prepared to deal with them in both mind and body, and reappeared with missionaries, traders, soldiers, administrators, police, and concessionaries. The missionaries, through Christianity, took up the assignment to prevent the Africans from their cultural ways, and at the same time implore them to lay down their "treasures in heaven where neither moth nor rust will destroy them."

As the Africans blindly followed these Christian gospels, the administrators, concessionaires, and traders were working overtime acquiring African mineral and land resources, looting the nations' arts, crafts, and destroying the peoples' home industries.

Africans were, of course, massively recruited under cheap labor to help exploit their land and themselves for the welfare of the Europeans both in

Europe and in Africa, and at the same time are forcibly broken up and disbanded after a few years by these colonialists and compelled to retire to their homes and villages where European exploitation was indirectly exercised through the corrupt chiefs they created in their place as the people's traditional chiefs, and their brainwashed academic elite. Through such actions they controlled African resentments against the European oppressors, and the conditions for mass organization against them was absorbed.

The colonialists failed to realize their activities in Africa had historical consequences that Africans or humanity at large might use in future to pass judgment on them. They failed to grasp the essential point that exploitation reproduces class structure in both among themselves, the colonizers and the colonized, and class society goes with the same theory of the strong surviving luxuriously at the expense of the weak while the weak remains in continuous abject poverty.

My concern here is, of course, that the African reaction to the European mindless exploitation of Africa and their use of colonialism destroyed African culture and human dignity and reduced them as servants and beggars in their own God-given land.

The reaction was rebellion and requests for what politicians call "independence" from the Europeans, freedom for the Africans to "do their own thing." (This is what Africans have now as freedom to exploit themselves.)

The Europeans were very much aware of what they gain from Africa, and to pull out like that without finding ways to continue the exploitation was unacceptable. Then they came up with the idea of joining the Commonwealth of nations, because they said that if Africa cut connections with their "mother countries," Africa would not have enough protection to keep off other European nations (the Europeans' have-nots). But the situation is on the reverse. Europe wanted Africans and Africa to continue the exploitation. Independence meant that African nations were free to associate themselves with any other nation or nations of the world. It therefore means also that Africans could allow other nations of the world to exploit their countries and even themselves, but at a price dictated by the Africans. It means also that the Africans could write their constitution and manipulate their laws as they like. It means at the same time that Africans can cheat themselves and their nations under the umbrella of the government while both the government authorities and the laws look unconcerned. So the Africans got the permit from their mother countries to practice "man's inhumanity to man" on themselves, and there is no one to control the rampage of the evil that is now out of bounds in African countries.

So Africans were relegated to that background of the new Euro-Africans. African gods protested, but the European god had taken hold of Africans who were once unquestioning subjects, and nobody was around to check the religion since it was the creation of the Europeans and all their exploitative tendencies.

The new religion that was designed to control Africans mentally asserted to them that it had brought them light to brighten their darkness.

Under this negotiated truth, truth can be bought at a price. The cheated consoles himself by falling back to the new religion; the Christian's reward is in heaven. There he would be given a place in the company of brother Christians who had kept in this world too much to the narrow path of virtue and righteousness.

To resist the colonialists meant being expelled from one's community. This meant the loss of the individual's human dignity, the loss of meaningful livelihood, and in most of the cases the loss of freedom of existence.

There are many examples of Africans who resisted these colonialists' ambitions to the extent of going to war, only to suffer defeat, be captured and disgraced among their subjects, and finally exiled from their homes, and in nearly all the cases they appointed to the Africans who regarded money and power in their places. Chinua Achobe points out in one of his urban novels, *Arrow of God*:

> The place where the Christians built their place of worship was not far from Ezeulu's compound. As he sat in his obi thinking of the Festival of the Pumpkin Leaves, he heard their bell: GOM, GOM, GOM, GOM, GOM. His mind turned from the festival to the new religion. He was not sure what to make of it. At first he had thought that since the white man had come with great power and conquest it was necessary that some people should learn the ways of his own deity. That was why he had agreed to send his son, Oduche, to learn the new ritual. He also wanted him to learn the white man's wisdom, for Ezeulu knew from what he saw of Wintabota and the stories he heard about his people that the white man was very wise.

> But now Ezeulu was becoming afraid that the new religion was like a leper. Allow him a handshake and he wants an embrace. Ezeulu had already spoken strongly to his son who was becoming more strange every day. Perhaps the time had come to bring him out again. But what would happen if, as many oracles had prophesied, the white man had come to take over the land and rule? In such a case it would be wise to have a man of your family in his band. As he thought about these things Oduche came from the inner compound wearing a white singlet and a towel which they had given him in school. Nwafo came out with him, admiring his singlet. Oduche saluted his father and set out for the mission because it was Sunday morning. The bell continued ringing in its sad monotone.

> Nwafo came back to the obi and asked his father whether he knew what the bell was saying. Ezeulu shook his head.

"Yes" said Ezeulu thoughtfully. "It tells them to leave their yam and their cocoyam, does it? Then it is singing the song of extermination."

They were interrupted by loud and confused talking inside the compound, and Nwafo ran out to see what it was. The voices were getting louder and Ezeulu who normally took no interest in women's shouting began to strain his ear. But Nwafo soon rushed back.

"Oduche's box is moving," he said, out of breath with excitement. The tumult in the compound grew louder. As usual the voice of Ezeulu's daughter, Akueke, stood out above all others.

"What is called 'Oduche's box is moving'?" He asked, rising with deliberate slowness to belie his curiosity.

"It is moving about the floor."

"There is nothing that a man will not hear nowadays." He went into his inner compound through the door at the back of his obi. Nwafo ran past him to the group of excited women outside his mother's hut. Akueke and Matefi did most of the talking. Nwafo's mother, Ugoye, was speechless. Now and again she rubbed her palms together and showed them to the sky.

Akueke turned to Ezeulu as soon as she saw him. "Father, come and see what we are seeing. This new religion…."

"Shut your mouth," said Ezeulu, who did not want anybody, least of all his own daughter, to question his wisdom in sending one of his sons to join the new religion.

The wooden box had been brought from the room where Oduche and Nwafo slept and placed in the central room of their mother's hut where people sat during the day and food was cooked.

The box, which was the only one of its kind in Ezeulu's compound, had a lock. Only people of the church had such boxes made for them by the mission carpenter and they were highly valued in Umuaro. Oduche's box was not actually moving, but it seemed to have something inside it struggling to be free. Ezeulu stood before it, wondering what to do. Whatever was inside the box became more violent and actually moved the box around. Ezeulu waited for it to calm down a little, bent down and carried the box outside. The women and children scattered in all directions.

"Whether it be bad medicine or good one, I shall see it today," he said as he carried the box at arms' length like a potent sacrifice. He did not pass through his obi, but took the door in the red earth wall of his compound. His second son, Obika, who had just come in followed him. Nwafo came closely behind Obika, and the women and children followed fearfully at a good distance. Ezeulu looked back and asked Obika to bring him a machete. He took the box right outside his compound and finally put it down by the side of the common footpath. He looked back and saw Nwafo and the women and children.

"Every one of you go back to the house. The inquisitive monkey gets a bullet in the face."

They moved back not into the compound but in front of the obi. Obika took a machete to his father who thought for a little while and put the machete aside and sent him for the spear used in digging up yams. The struggling inside the box was as fierce as ever. For a brief moment Ezeulu wondered whether the wisest thing was not to leave the box there until its owner returned. But what would it mean? That he, Ezeulu, was afraid of whatever power his son had imprisoned in a box. Such a story must never be told of the priest of Ulu.

He took the spear from Obika and wedged its thin end between the box and its lid. Obika tried to take the spear from him, but he would not hear it.

"Stand aside," he told him. "What do you think is fighting inside? Two cocks?" He clenched his teeth in an effort to lever the top open. It was not easy, and the old priest was covered in sweat by the time he succeeded in forcing the box. What they saw was enough to blind a man. Ezeulu was speechless. The women and children who had watched from afar came running down. Ezeulu's neighbor, Anosi, who was passing by branched in, and soon a big crowd had gathered. In the broken box lay an exhausted royal python.

"May the Great Deity forbid," said Anosi.

"An abomination has happened," said Akueke.

Matefi said "If this is medicine, may it lose its potency."

Ezeulu let the spear fall from his hand. "Where is Oduche?" he asked. No one answered. "I said, where is Oduche?" He asked. No one answered. "I said, where is Oduche?" His voice was terrible.

Nwafo said he had gone to church. The sacred python now raised its head above the edge of the box and began to move in its dignified and unhurried way.

"Today I shall kill the boy with my own hands," said Ezeulu as he picked up the machete which Obika had brought at first.

"May the Great Deity forbid such a thing," said Anosi.

"I have said it."

Oduche's mother began to cry, and the other women joined her. Ezeulu walked slowly back to his obi with the machete. The royal python slid away into the bush.

"What is the profit of crying?" Anosi asked Ugoye. "Won't you find where your son is and tell him not to return home today?"

"He has spoken the truth, Ugoye," said Matefi. "Send him away to your kinsmen. We are fortunate the python is not dead."

"You are indeed fortunate," said Anosi to himself as he continued on his way to Umunneora to buy seed-yams from his friend. "I have already said that what this new religion will bring to Umuaro wears a hat on its head." As he went he stopped and told anyone he met what Ezeulu's son had done. Before midday the story had reached the ears of Ezidemili whose deity, Idemili, owned the royal python.

This quotation from *Things Fall Apart* is an imagination of Achebe as a writer. The case of Nana of the Delta, was not an imagination.

Nana had risen to become the leader of his people, and had controlled the trade in his area. Nana knew nothing of the British, until one day he saw himself and his people being given orders by the British. He resisted the orders, and led his subjects to resist the colonialists also.

The resistance led to war. Nana was defeated, tried, and exiled to Gold Coast (Ghana). After the British had tamed him in the exile for some years, he was brought back to his kingdom, where he later died.

Nana was lucky to come home alive and lived for some years among his people before he died. The case of the Jaja of Opobo, the slave who became king among his people, was different.

Jaja had learned from experience that he would reign and live longer if he stayed friendly with the British. He was of course friendly by nature and had hoped to use the British to attract trade to Opobo, and finally to use the British support to build his new state of Opobo.

But with all the good gestures towards the British, the British were not satisfied. They found ways to make trouble with him. They captured the king and exiled him to St. Vincent. E. J. Alagoa documented the trial of the Nigerian king in his pamphlet, "Jaja of Opobo."

Unlike the case of Nana of the Delta, the British tried to consolidate themselves at Nana's kingdom but:

> "In Opobo, sending Jaja away did not do any good for the British companies. Some of them went upriver to start trading stations at Ohambele, but trade was not good. By 1893 the British decided to return to Opobo. There they again started to buy all their palm oil and other goods from Opobo traders, just as they had done before the trade war with Jaja."

In St. Vincent, Jaja tried to live as happily as he could, but he longed to return to Opobo. He constantly wrote to the British government asking to be allowed to return. Many questions about him were asked in the British Parliament. Several members of the Parliament believed the Accra trial had been unfair and that Acting Consul Johnston had behaved very badly when he tricked Jaja into attending the meeting with him. One member of Parliament complained that the saying "to lie like an Englishman" had become common on the West African coast.

Even Jaja was still a threat to the British when he was in exile. The British injustice to Nigerians was revealed during the Jaja's trial in Ghana. This injustice preyed on the conscience of the British Parliament, who yielded to the king's request to be returned to his kingdom. But the British who were in Jaja's kingdom knew how powerful Jaja was among his people, so they planned.

At last, in 1891, Jaja signed an agreement saying he would not give trouble to the British government if he returned to Opobo. He started to sail home, but he was now old and weak. He died on the way home at the island of Tenerife on July 7, 1891.

And so Nana of Delta and Jaja lost their kingdoms to the colonialist. They suffered the humiliation among their people, the loss of their dignity, and even their lives. Even though Nana got back to his kingdom, he was a "broken spirit." He only came back to die at home. Jaja's age hurried upon him and he died before he could reach Opobo.

Oba Ovonramwen, in his resisting the colonialists ambition to usurp his power in his Bini kingdom, suffered the loss of his dignity, his kingdom, and was exiled also like the Nana of the Delta and Jaja of Opobo. It can be added also that his suffering was worst, for he could have believed that his subject he brought up made a chief and even gave one of his daughters to marry Obaseki of Benin, while he rotted in exile. Philip Aigbano Igbafe narrates this in his pamphlet "Obaseki of Benin," and politely played down Obaseki's betrayal of his Oba and his use of the British to usurp the leadership role of Oba Ovonramwen.

Up to this time, the Obas of Benin had ordered the social, political, and economic life of their kingdom as they saw fit. In matters of trade, the Oba not only had a monopoly of certain items of merchandise, but he also decided on what terms non-Bini traders were to carry on trade in his domain. The most famous non-Bini traders were the Itsekiri who lived along the coast. They were the middlemen between the Bini and the European traders at the coast. The Oba imposed a tax on the Itsekiri. They had to pay a certain sum in goods to the Oba before they were allowed to trade. The sum was fixed from time to time by the Oba. The Itsekiri themselves did the same thing to European traders who traded in their kingdom. These Europeans had to pay "comey" or dues to the Itsekiri ruler before they could trade. Yet the Itsekiri complained when the Oba of Benin did the same thing to them.

The Itsekiri would perhaps not have complained loudly if British traders in the area had not encouraged them to do so. All through the 1880s the European traders tried hard to get the Oba to lift the dues he imposed on non-Bini traders. They also tried to get him to put an end to the practice whereby he stopped trade flowing to the coast if the traders did not pay the dues he imposed. Despite the efforts of the Europeans—the British Vice Consuls as well as the Royal Niger Company—the Oba refused to change the system. The European attitude was of course purely selfish. The Itsekiri middlemen wanted to make more profit at the expense of the Oba.

One year after Gallway was stationed in the Benin River, he visited Benin to try and get the Oba to sign a "protection treaty" with the British. Part of this treaty provided for free trade in the Oba's domain. If the Oba had signed this treaty, he would have lost the right to impose dues on foreign traders, and the right to close the trade routes when the dues were not paid or when for some other reason the Oba was dissatisfied with prevailing trade conditions. The Oba was in any case suspicious of Gallway's intentions and so refused to sign the treaty.

But some of his chiefs signed it. Naturally, the Oba continued to control trade the way he had always done. The British authorities now complained that the Oba was breaking the terms of his treaty. Gallway, in a report written in 1893, complained about the Oba's power over trade and stated the British would not be able to reap full benefits from the Benin territories unless the Oba was removed from his throne.

Nothing, however, happened immediately after this report. For one thing, the British were fully occupied in 1894 with the great Itsekiri middlemen, Chief Nana, against whom they waged a war that year. Nana was bombarded and eventually exiled because he held too great control of the trade on the Benin River and Warri districts. The Oba of Benin was to suffer a similar fate.

It was with a view to get the Oba to change his ways that the Acting Consul-General Phillips decided to visit Benin in 1897. Phillips sent a message to the Oba informing him of his intention to visit Benin. The Oba sent back a reply that it was festival time and no foreigner was allowed in Benin during the festivals. Despite this reply and despite the advice of Itsekiri traders who knew Bini customs well, Phillips decided to go ahead with his trip to Benin.

The Oba got to hear of Phillips' visit from the spies he placed on the route. Phillips' decision to go to Benin despite the Oba's refusal to let him come gave his trip a sinister look. If he was coming as a friend why was he ignoring the message sent him by the Oba, who was to be his host? He summoned a meeting of his chiefs to discuss the situation. It was clear the Europeans were trying to reach Benin by force, and it was decided they must be stopped. The chiefs dispersed and sent their soldiers under the leadership of the Ologbose and other war chiefs to the route Phillips was to take. This order was clear. Phillips and his party were to be prevented from reaching Benin. They did not reach Benin.

At the public meeting of the Benin chief mentioned above, Chief Ologbose, who was second in command of the Benin army next to Ezomo, was chosen to head the party to guard the approach road to Benin City. Many other war-chiefs in Benin went with him, the most prominent of whom were Obakhaveaye, Obayuwana, Igupbasoyemi, Obaradesagdon, and Ohebo. They chose a narrow section of the road near the village of Ugbine where a party could only walk in a single file.

The Bini soldiers laid a careful ambush, waiting for the arrival of Phillips's party. They were armed with guns and cutlasses. Chiefs who did not personally go to Ugbine sent soldiers. In this latter group was Oshodi, Ihaza, Ayobahan, Obaseki, Ine, Ehanire, Obasuaye and Ehonodo. Unfortunately for the party of Europeans and carriers, Phillips did not have the patience to wait for the return of Idiaghe, the messenger he sent to the Oba to inform him of the party's refusal to defer their visit. Phillips and his party hastily set out from Ughoton.

Near Ugbine, Phillips sent a messenger in advance to prepare a resting place for the night in that village. This messenger found Bini soldiers and chiefs in ambush; while he was discussing the wisdom or folly of ambushing the expedition with Chief Ologbose's soldiers, Phillips' party arrived at Ugbine. After entering deep into the ambush in a long single line, the party was fired upon by Bini soldiers. It was easy to fire at members of the expedition at close range. Benin soldiers killed several members of the party. Those who died in the ambush included the leader of the expedition, James R. Phillips, Peter Copland-Crawford, Arthur Maling, Kenneth Campbell,

Robert Eliott, Harry Powis, and Thomas Gordon. Only two of the white men, Alan Boisragon and Mr. Locke, escaped. Those of the party who did not die of gunshot wounds immediately had their heads cut off later with cutlasses by the Bini soldiers.

Phillips and six of the white men who accompanied him together with some one hundred twenty-four of the two hundred fifty carriers who went with the party were killed by the Bini soldiers. This was on 4 January 1897.

Early in 1897 the British Government decided to avenge the death of Phillips and his party. A land and sea attack was planned against Benin. Nine ships of the British navy steamed into the Benin River District. All the soldiers of the protectorate were also assembled. On 10 February 1897 the attack on Benin began. On 18 February British rockets set the Oba's palace ablaze and the Oba and his principle chiefs were forced to flee. Soon after, the British took Benin. The fall of Benin in February 1897 was to completely change the career of Chief Agho Obaseki.

Obaseki, as one of the Bini chiefs and particularly as one very close to the Oba, had played his own part in the events which led to the fall of Benin. He and the other chiefs agreed that Phillips' party was to be prevented from reaching Benin. In fact, Obaseki, together with others like the Oshodi, Ihaza, Ayobahan, Ehondo, and Ehanire, sent their fighting men with the Oglobose to the Ughoton-Ugbin-Benin road to ensure that Phillips' party was not allowed to reach Benin. Others, like Obaseki, who had received newly created titles, actually went to the front to join in the fighting. This was true of Obayuwana, Obaradesagbon, and Obakhavbaye. Obaseki stayed behind to be close to the Oba. During the British offensive against Benin, Obaseki again played his part as a faithful chief. He placed all his fighting force at the Oba's service. Up to the time of the fall of Benin, therefore, Obaseki had done nothing to suggest disloyalty to the Oba and his friend. If any proof of this statement is required, it is to be found in the fact that when, in the face of British rocket fire, the Oba decided to escape, Obaseki was one of the trusted chiefs who accompanied the Oba.

After the Oba and his chiefs had fled the capital, the British occupied the city. Many of the inhabitants followed the example of their Oba and fled. The first few weeks of the British occupation were spent in trying to get the people to return to Benin. The people and some of the chiefs began to return when they found the British were no longer killing Binis or firing rockets. It was in this situation that in April 1897 the Oba sent Obaseki from Erua to Benin City to see how things were going and to report back to him. Obaseki obeyed the instructions of his Oba and went to Benin. While he was in Benin the British discovered his true identity and prevented him from going back to the Oba. A man as near to the Oba as Obaseki could help the British to re-establish normal life in Benin. The drift from the Oba had begun without any real plan by Obaseki.

The British began to use Obaseki's presence in Benin to attract other chiefs to return. In the second half of May the Ezomo and Iyase returned to Benin. Other chiefs like Obahiagbon, Oshodi, Uwangwe, and Osague returned and submitted to the British. Villages and communities also began to submit. Life in Benin began to return to normal.

Very wisely, and with a view to create the impression that the people were to be ruled by their own chiefs, Alfred Turner (the British political resident), appointed a Council of Benin chiefs to govern the city and Benin Territories. The Oshodi and Osague were among those first appointed to serve on the council. In July and again in September 1897 six other chiefs including Obaseki were appointed. By the end of the year most of the chiefs who had returned and whose loyalty was not in question were appointed to the council. The Ezomo, Ine, Imaran, and Uwangwe were among the last group appointed.

By August 1897, Oba Ovonramwen was beginning to feel isolated. Most of his chiefs, including the trusted Obaseki, had submitted (willingly or otherwise) to the British. What was the point of his holding out alone? So on 6 August 1897 he, too, surrendered. On 1 September 1897, the trial of the Oba and those chiefs who were actually present at the scene of attack on Phillips' party began in Benin. Chief Agho Obaseki was one of those present in the Native Council for this trial. The trial was conducted by Sir Ralph Moor, who had succeeded Macdonald as head of the administration of the Niger Coast Protectorate. Ralph Moor declared the Oba guilty and deposed him. For Obaseki, who watched the proceedings as a member of the Native Council, this must have been a very painful experience. His friend and ruler was deposed by the white man. Later, when the Oba refused to go on a tour of the Protectorate suggested by Moor, he was exiled to Calabar.

The removal of the Oba from the Benin scene created a completely new political situation. The one man to whom Obaseki owed a special loyalty had been removed. It must have pained the Oba to see friends like Obaseki sit in the Native Council dumbly while he was sentenced to deportation and exile. But there was little that Obaseki could have done except volunteer to go into exile without his Oba. Self-interest prevented that supreme sacrifice for a friend who had done so much for him. That was a weakness of character; but a weakness common to many men. In the new situation now created, Obaseki did not see any reason why he should worry about anything except his own interests. And in promoting these interests he rose to become the leading figure in Bini that time until his death in 1920.

Like other chiefs, Obaseki was appointed paramount chief. Once again Obaseki went to work with all the energy and ability for which he had become known. His area was seen by the British to be the best administered. He was always quick to supply carriers for British political officers reported favorably on Obaseki, who was described as being prominent in supplying laborers for public works, and capable of maintaining law and order in his area of authority.

In terms of material wealth, Obaseki also did well for himself. He was lucky his area contained timber when trees began to be felled for timber; he as paramount chief received one-third of the royalties which were paid by those who felled trees. The remaining two-thirds were supposed to be shared by the towns and villages, although in practice the paramount chief took even some of this share. When payment was made for public works the paramount chief also took one-third of this, and as Obaseki was always in the lead in providing men for public works, he made money from these as well. In addition to such sources of wealth, Obaseki was also often given government contracts to build court houses, quarters for clerks, police barracks, and prisons, as well as contracts for the construction of roads and clearing of bush for the erection of telephone lines. From such contracts Obaseki made a great deal of money in comparison with other chiefs. He won these contracts because the British government trusted his efficiency and ability to get work done satisfactorily. The more of such works he undertook, the wealthier he became. Obaseki thus combined wealth and increasing political authority in Benin. Despite the protests of other chiefs in 1899, Obaseki was still regarded by the British.

1. An agreement between Agho Obaseki and the Benin District Commissioner. The text is as follows:

An agreement made this ninth day of March 1904 between the District Commissioner Benin City on behalf of the Government of Southern Nigeria on the one part and Chief Obaseki of Benin City called herein the Contractor on the other part. The Contractor agrees to build on a site to be pointed out, a row of houses seventeen in number, Kekry style, made of mud and wood with a mat roof, in addition to the 3 Bini houses already nearing completion, of a dimension of 14' x 14' inclusive of a 6' veranda for the sum of sixty pounds. The District Commissioner on behalf of the Government of South Nigeria agrees to pay the said sum of sixty pounds provided the houses are ready for habitation on April 14th, 1904.

Should any one or one or more of the houses not be fit for habitation on the aforesaid date the Contractor agrees to pay on each house so incomplete for every day that they remain unfit for habitation the sum of one shilling. The Contractor also agrees that the District Commissioner or his assign decision as to whether the said Houses are finished be final.

Signed this 9th day of March 1904.

Witness

J. E. Ihaya   A. R. Mytton   Chief Obaseki

                     Asst. D.C.   his/mark

                     For D.C.

As the leading chief in Benin, as was proved even he was selected to lead the Benin delegation of chiefs to an agricultural show in Lagos in 1906.

By this time other chiefs had become extremely jealous of him and angry about his position. At the head of the opposition to Obaseki was Aiguobasimwin, the eldest son of the exiled Oba and the future Oba Eweka II. Aiguobasimwin no doubt felt that the leading position held by Obaseki should naturally belong to him as the son of the exiled Oba. He was supported by a large number of the minor chiefs who had virtually no say under the British, as well as many of the more important chiefs who felt their positions diminished by the powers and wealth of Obaseki.

The way the opposition went to work was to begin a secret movement which was to fight for the return of the exiled Oba. Meetings were held at night, and oaths of secrecy were taken by the members. Many villages and towns joined the movement. Members began to collect money for the struggle. The town meetings started to try cases between individuals as if they were native courts. Villages refused to pay their tribute to their chiefs and paid it to the movement instead. It looked as if British authority itself was being challenged. In September 1906 those organizing the movement invited Obaseki to join. Other major chiefs invited included Obayagbon, Iyamu, and Ayobahan.

Obaseki was put in a difficult position by the invitation. If the movement was to fight for the restoration of his friend and benefactor Ovonramwen, could he really refuse to join? On the other hand, if he joined the movement, his support might well lead to the British considering the recall of the Oba. If the Oba returned would he, Obaseki, still enjoy his present influence, position, power and wealth? What if the British refused to let the Oba return and crushed the movement? These questions must have worried Obaseki. Once again, as in 1897, he chose to protect his own interests.

And so Obaseki refused to join. Having refused to join he and three other chiefs, Obayogbon, Iyamu, and Ayobahan, informed the District Commissioner about the movement. The British reacted quickly. Troops were poured into Benin in September 1906 and all the villages concerned once more submitted. Tribute which had not been paid was now paid, and what looked like a political rebellion was crushed.

In the process of crushing the movement the British tried to find out what was at the root of it. The other chiefs came out quite openly against Obaseki. Obaseki, they argued, was junior in rank to many of them. Yet he had been helped by the British to become the most senior and respected chief in Benin. The British political officers were in the habit of listening only to Obaseki in matters concerning Benin. Once Obaseki had spoken no other voice mattered. Besides, Obaseki was exploiting his influence with the British to make a great deal of money for himself. It was typical of the relationship between Obaseki and the government, which did nothing to alter the position. The other chiefs were merely told that Obaseki would not be dragged down to their level.

On that contrary, the British even increased Obaseki's influence after 1906. In 1908 he was appointed paramount chief over Benin City itself as well as the immediate neighborhood. In other words, Obaseki became the ruler (subject, of course, to British control) of the Oba's capital itself. It was a great honor. Obaseki had virtually become an uncrowned Oba.

In 1910 the British decided to pay Obaseki a salary (subsidy as it used to be called) to 40 lira per annum in addition to what he otherwise received as paramount chief. This sum was increased to 60 lira in 1913. The provincial commissioner justified the increase by arguing that the chiefs of Epe, Shamu, Ife, and Ijebu-Ode were receiving salaries of 72, 100, 100, and 200 respectively, and yet were in no way comparable to Obaseki who was thus judged to be more powerful and useful than crowned Obas of Yorubaland like the Oni of Ife and the Awujale of Ijebu-Ode. Over and above this regular pay, Obaseki received gifts in September and December of 1911 for "meritorious services."

While the British thus honored a loyal and efficient servant, the Oba Ovonramwen, still in exile, recognized the success in public life of this one time friend by giving his daughter Orinmwiame to Obaseki in marriage in 1912. To marry an Oba's daughter was an honor reserved to men of stature and success in Benin society.

Between 1897 and 1914, when an Oba was restored to Benin, Obaseki thus established great influence and power for himself. So great was this power that it was difficult, as we shall see in the next section, to reduce Obaseki's effective position despite the installation of Aiguobasimwin as Oba Eweka II in 1914.

Like the Jaja of Opobo, Oba Ovonramwen died in exile and his death took the same pattern of "sudden heart attack" which came out of the blue skies at a desperate time for the British to solidify their installation of colonialism in the kingdoms: This again was politely documented by Igbafe and his "Obaseki of Benin."

From Paramount Chief to Iyase of Bini

Although the movement of 1906 which had among its aims the restoration of the Oba of Benin was crushed, the idea of the Oba being recalled from exile did not die as a consequence. One reason why the movement had reached such a height in 1906 was that Chief Nana, who had been in exile in the Gold Coast since 1894, was allowed to return in that year. His return made the Bini feel their own Oba might also be allowed to return. Various petitions were forwarded asking the British to allow the Oba to return. But the British would not hear of Oba Ovonramwen returning to Benin.

In 1914, however, southern and northern Nigeria became amalgamated, and Sir Frederick Lugard was appointed governor general of the new Nigeria. Lugard had been high commissioner (i.e. governor) of Northern Nigeria from 1900 to 1908. During that period he had ruled Northern Nigeria by means of a system known as Indirect Rule.

By this system, Lugard recognized the emirs of Northern Nigeria as native authorities with powers to run local government. Under the emirs were the judges of the native courts, district headmen and village headmen. A council made up of various titleholders advised the emirs. The emirs were allowed to collect taxes from their people and to keep about half the taxes so collected, while giving the other half to the British government. With their share of the tax, they maintained themselves, paid their subordinate officers, and carried out public works within their areas of authority. The emirs had their own police force and their own prisons. British political officers supervised the emir and his staff in all aspects of local government.

When Lugard became governor general of Nigeria, he decided to extend to the south the system of local government which had been described above. As he looked round the south, Lugard found that Benin was one area into which he could introduce the Indirect Rule system. The Oba of Benin appeared to Lugard to be very near in status and power to the emirs of the north. There already existed districts over which headmen could be appointed. But the Oba of Benin was in exile and the system Lugard was seeking to introduce could not work without an Oba. It thus became necessary that an Oba should be found for Benin.

According to Benin custom, it was impossible to install another Oba while Ovonramwen was alive. The British political officers were dead against Ovonramwen returning to Benin as Oba. It looked as if there might be a crisis in a situation where Lugard wanted an Oba but in which his subordinates in Benin would not have the existing Oba and could not install a new one. Fortunately for the British, Oba Ovonramwen died on 13 January 1914.

The death of Oba Ovonramwen gave room for the installation of Oba Eweka Mwen's son Aiguobasimwin as the Obaseki of Benin used his British friends to weaken his authority in his kingdom. Igbafe points out this politely in his "Obaseki of Benin."

The death of Ovonramwen left the way clear for the appointment and installation of a new Oba of Benin. It was here that Obaseki came in once again. As soon as James Watt, the British Commissioner in charge of Benin Province got the news of Ovonramwen's death, he summoned Obaseki to a private interview. He asked Obaseki about the laws of the succession in Benin. Obaseki was honest enough to admit that according to Bini tradition the Oba had to be succeeded by his eldest son. James Watt then inquired whether a commoner could not become an Oba and whether, as in Yoruba practice, another royal house could not provide a candidate for the Benin throne. Obaseki again truthfully answered that such a practice would be against Bini tradition.

The interview revealed quite clearly the thoughts going on in the mind of James Watt. Obaseki had been the most loyal and efficient servant of the British. Might it be possible to get him installed as Oba of Benin and so make him, in the new system that Lugard was seeking to introduce, head of the Benin Native Administration? Obaseki, too, must have seen the possibilities but had truthfully told the British officer what the custom was. The question that now arose was: would custom be upheld or would it be overlooked in order to honor Obaseki?

James Watt did not immediately make a decision. He summoned Aiguobasimwin, Eson, Ezomo, and Ero, together with Obaseki, to yet another interview to discuss the situation. Surprisingly, this time Obaseki answered, in response to the question of who should be Oba, that he was prepared to do anything the commissioner directed. He was backed by Ezomo, who said that even if the commissioner decided that a woman should become the Oba, he would be ready to accept such an Oba. Chief Ero, however, stuck out for tradition. Only the late Oba's eldest son, he told the Commissioner, could become Oba. After Obaseki's clear stand at the private interview earlier on, his wavering stand at this public interview is evidence that he was already responding to the temptations of acquiring the supreme office in Benin. He was probably secretly advised by other chiefs who were relying on him, should he had been accustomed to giving orders. It was too much perhaps to think he would want to stop giving orders and begin to take orders from Aiguobasimwin, who was the rightful candidate for the throne. Power was to break Bini traditions.

James Watt, still anxious to do what he could for his servant, refused even at this stage to reach a decision. He continued to investigate. He asked that Oni of Ife and other rulers their views about the succession practice in Benin. Meanwhile Lugard himself ordered an investigation into the matter. At the end of all of these investigations, even James Watt was forced to recommend that Aiguobasimwin should succeed his father as Oba.

Native administration system into Benin. The chief organs of this system of local government were a central native authority made up of the Oba and a council of eight chiefs, native courts, district heads, and a treasury into which the revenue of the Native Administration was paid. The Iyase was in theory supposed to be the Oba's chief advisor and second-in-command. In practice, as we shall see, the Iyase completely overshadowed the Oba.

Obaseki's position in their new setup was guaranteed from the very beginning. The new Oba was not allowed to enjoy all the power which Obas before him had enjoyed. He could no longer appoint chiefs unless this was approved by the British District Officer. He had to seek the permission of the same officer before he could grant permits for hunters to kill elephants for their tusks or before he could control foodstuff prices in the markets of his domains. He could not even receive presents from loyal subjects without the permission of the district officer. The control of the forests and land which had formerly been possessed by the Oba in times past was no longer completely in the hands of the new Oba. He was thus a very weakened Oba who was now head of the Benin Native Administration. The Iyase, on the other hand, was a man who had built up a great deal of power in the period before the installation of the Oba. Was this man likely to lose any of his previous powers? It did not look as if he would. If anything, the British administrative officers believed the Oba could only carry on his functions if he listened to the Iyase. In other words, although there was now an Oba, it was the Iyase who was regarded by the British as the backbone of the Native Administration. As a senior British officer put it, "As long as Oba Eweka follows the advice of the Iyase, he will not go wrong."

Obaseki thus came to dominate the working of the new system. It is true there was an Oba's council. This council was to act as an executive as well as judicial body. It was responsible for seeing to the day-to-day government of the Benin Division. It heard appeals from the native courts in the other towns and villages. The council was to advise the Oba in matters to do with the selection of district heads, native court members, ward or quarter heads, and village heads, as well as the control of the revenues and the forests. If the council had been allowed to function, perhaps Obaseki's powers would not have grown as they did. As it was, the council did very little real work. The district officers formed the habit of discussing issues with Obaseki, the Iyase, and occasionally with the Oba, and merely keeping the council informed of decisions reached. In other words, the Oba and Iyase tended to replace the council, and as the Iyase was the one trusted by the British, it was he who was consulted most by the district officer.

In the last pages we spoke about the appointment of paramount chiefs. Under the new Native Administration system there were no paramount chiefs. Instead district heads were appointees. Benin Division was broken up into four districts–Benin, Siluko, Orhonigbe and Igbanke. Of these four districts, Benin District, with an area of nearly 4,000 square miles and a population of some 84,000 was the most important. It was not therefore surprising that Agho Obaseki, the Iyase, was appointed district head of Benin District in 1916. He began on a salary of 550 pounds per annum and was earning 800 pounds by the time of his death in 1920. The other District Heads were Inehe for Siluko, Oshodi for Orhonigbe, and Osula for Igbanke.

The district heads enjoyed great powers. They were automatically members of the Oba's central council. They collected from their districts as well as rents and other fees paid by non-Binis who exploited the oil palm trees in the division. After the introduction of direct taxation, they supervised the collection of this tax. They, like the paramount chiefs of the earlier period, supervised public works like the building of roads, bridges, markets, and so on. They were responsible for seeing that law and order were maintained in their areas of authority. The district heads were thus very important persons. Obaseki was even more important than the others. This was because in addition to being district head he had the title of Iyase and held the post of chief advisor to the Oba, a position of power and influence. He was also greatly respected by the British administrative officers, who sought his advice on virtually every issue.

As if all this was not enough, Obaseki was appointed permanent president of three native courts—Benin, Ekenwan, and Enor. Under the Native Administration system, these courts were very important indeed. They were not just courts of law. They were also the native authorities in the areas over which they had legal jurisdiction. In other words, apart from trying cases, they were also responsible for maintaining law and order, supervising public works, looking after markets, and generally taking charge of the day-to-day governing of the towns and villages whose members attended the courts. Because of this fact the native court members became very important figures in their villages or towns. The villagers or townspeople always did everything to be on friendly terms with the court members. Often, court members were given presents. Some people were even prepared to let their children do manual labor for such court members. They did so that such court members would use their positions to benefit their friends. If ordinary court members were such important figures in their communities, it is easy to imagine how important the president of the court himself would be. And Obaseki was president of three different courts including that of Benin. Apart from his other sources of influence and power, being president of the Benin native court made Obaseki easily the most important figure in Benin City itself, the British officers excepted.

Both as district head and as president of three native courts in 1915, the British district officer reported on Obaseki: "The Benin City native court under the presidency of Chief Obaseki has worked with great satisfaction. There have been but few complaints and appeals from the decisions of this court." It is difficult to be sure whether Obaseki was as efficient as this kind of report painted him. After all, everybody knew that he was the friend of the British officers. Anyone who complained too much about him would probably get into the bad books of the district officer. What was the point of appealing against the judgment of Obaseki when the district officer who would hear the appeal was Obaseki's friend? On the other hand, Obaseki knew he was the friend of the British because he was loyal and carried out instructions faithfully. He would, therefore, probably have tried to carry out his duties efficiently. It is probable, however, that he did abuse his powers and many offices. That the reports of the British administrative officers said little or nothing about such abuse of office shows they may have been prejudiced in favor of Obaseki. Just before his death the Bini chiefs were to make a long list of his misdeeds in a petition to the governor general.

The system of district heads was unpopular with the people, with the other chiefs, and with the Oba. The district heads were so powerful the people could do very little to avoid being oppressed. It is said the district heads often collected more tribute from the people than was approved. They seized young girls as wives for themselves or their relations and friends. Yams and goats were demanded by the district heads or their agents from the towns and villages. The people were forced to work on the farms of the district heads without pay. For these reasons the district heads were unpopular with the ordinary people.

There were only four district heads. This meant many of the former paramount chiefs lost office. As for the town and village heads, they came under the control of the new district heads. In other words, where before many of the people had enjoyed power, power was now monopolized by four people only. The chiefs therefore hated the system which deprived them of their former influence and power.

In pre-British days the appointment of chiefs was the responsibility of the Oba. However, the new Oba could no longer appoint chiefs without the approval of the district officer. The appointment of the district heads was therefore not the sole responsibility of the Oba. Besides, once these district heads had been appointed, the Oba could not, on his own authority, dismiss them from office. So while the district heads were enjoying power, the Oba was losing power. This was enough to make the district heads unpopular with the Oba. Added to that was the fact that the district heads used their position to make themselves wealthy and to oppress the people. Deprived of his former power to remove or transfer territorial chiefs whose positions had now been taken by the district heads, the Oba adopted a policy of non-cooperation. He often ignored the district heads and dealt directly through royal messengers with villages under their charge. This weakened the position and prestige of the district heads, as well as exposing their abuse of office. And so the district officers were made aware of the misdeeds of their servants, and decided on a policy of rotation of district heads. The Oba thus achieved indirectly what he could not achieve through a direct exercise of his powers. There was, however, one district head who could not be moved even through this strategy. This was Obaseki. Obaseki was reported to be efficient. Nobody accused him of abuse of office. So the Oba could find no official reason for moving him. This fact merely shows how powerless the Oba was when compared with one who was supposed to be only his second-in-command. Obaseki was too powerful for the Oba.

The British did not make any attempt to hide the fact that they regarded Obaseki as the most important figure in Benin and as a virtual head of the Native Administration. In 1915, when it was decided to send someone to study how the Native Administration worked in Ilorin, it was Obaseki the British sent. Again in 1917, when a delegation was sent to Zaria to study the system there, Obaseki headed the delegation. It was thus quite clear Obaseki was regarded as easily the most important political figure in the Benin Native Administration. It was too much to expect all this power would not go to Obaseki's head. As a result, Obaseki grew arrogant and even dictatorial. There was one occasion when Obaseki even questioned the Oba's right to give judgment in a case in Siluko without consulting him. Yet Siluko as not in the Benin District, of which Obaseki was head. Even the British were forced to admit at least on one occasion that Obaseki had grown "certainly more dictatorial and arrogant in his behavior." It was not, however, until 1920 that this arrogant behavior began to be questioned by both the Bini chiefs and the British.

In 1917 Obaseki decided to become a Christian. We cannot say whether Obaseki was genuinely converted or whether he was just playing politics. Anyway, until his death he attended the St. Matthew's C.M.S. Church in Benin. Obaseki's becoming a Christian raised important issues for Oba. It meant, for example, that he could not participate in the palace rituals which were regarded as non-Christian. It was a matter of grave importance for the Iyase to be absent from important palace rituals. However, in 1918 the Oba tried to create a crisis. He refused to perform the opening ceremonies of the new yam festival. Because the Oba refused to do this, the ordinary people could not perform their own ceremonies. This meant that the yams could not be harvested. This began to create hardship. The people protested and the British stepped in. The Oba argued he required the presence of the Iyase at the ceremonies and that since the Iyase could not attend because he was a Christian he could not carry out the rituals. In other words the Oba put the whole blame on Obaseki the Iyase. The British officers refused to accept the Oba's explanation and not only forced the Oba to carry out the ceremonies but also made him publicly apologize to Obaseki. This was perhaps Obaseki's greatest triumph: the Oba of Benin apologizing to his Iyase. This would never have happened but for the British. The Oba had no choice. Not only did he apologize; he even went as far as demonstrating his reconciliation with the powerful Iyase by giving his daughter, Princess Ebose, in marriage to Obaseki. Now Ovonramwen's son, as Oba Eweka II, had also married his daughter to Obaseki. Obaseki was obviously doing very well for himself. But he was also making enemies. Soon the enemies would come together against him. And with that drawing together of his enemies, Obaseki's end was near.

This is how the colonialists remade African societies, changed their directions, redirected the nation's heart against itself. It was an adventure on the side of the Europeans, and this is why it is painful to watch Africans as they are today.

When these colonialists inherited Africa at the Berlin conference in 1885 as the gift from their god, groups of Africans with their own cultures were forced under one flag by the colonialists, and these people, became legally what they are not historically. They were forced to turn away from their ways to maintain their destinies to that of working for and maintaining the destinies of the European countries. Those who resisted this colonial ambition to use Africans to maintain their destinies suffered the ugly fates which became those of the Nana of the Delta, Jaja of Opobo, and the Oba Ovonramwen of Bini in Nigeria.

The Europeans told themselves, the world, and the Africans they had to take such steps because they were civilizing the savages. This civilization is what may be modernization through slavery, and when they resisted, had to come through the treaties or genocide - colonialism - humanizing the savages.

This is how they installed themselves in Africa, exploited and alienated Africans from themselves and their lands, and built colonial towns which served as clearing houses between Europe and Africa. Then they imposed new rules, new institutions, new histories, and in time turned Africans to "new men with new values"—the values which supported the European economy and lifestyle while the new value left Africans in poverty and squalor.

These new values led Africans to Europeanize themselves to be admitted into the "exalted" European civilization. This ambition changed the African cultures in such a drastic way that Africans by the natural laws which govern their environments cannot become Europeans and therefore cannot use European culture to sustain themselves yet still cannot appreciate their cultures and therefore cannot use them to make life meaningful for themselves.

Many Africans, out of frustration, stupidity, or ignorance, still hope against hope to take advantage of the new history with its new culture. They studied it, memorized it, and are so efficient in it that they do teach it, yet they are unable to use it.

They had seen the new culture as the surest and fastest way to get ahead in their environment. Africans took advantage of the new value in the wage-labor economy new money and entered the colonial culture as the alternative to the values and rewards of the traditional economy. This has been the force—the new money, the new culture which has controlled the Africans ever since Europeans imposed colonialism on them.

What African was as Equiano described, or as can be remembered, changed to become the lifestyle with which Africans now measure themselves with job differentiation and education to determine their levels and degrees of Europeanizing themselves.

Here hinges the cure of the problems now eating down African societies. How does one tell the modern African high school graduate, a degree holder from bachelor degrees to the "Ph.D.'s," that he is not civilized or not cultured or that his knowledge and his behavior are the cankerworms destroying Africa? How can one tell African governments manned by the same Europeanized Africans that they are perpetuating the nations' problems by institutionalizing this Europeanized Africans and his Western education? How can one tell Africans that the education which built Europe and the "new world"–the United States of America–is detrimental for the progress of Africa?

I must correct something here by giving this example on education, or the purpose of this book may be misunderstood. Education is acquired knowledge. It is like a well-sharpened knife or a loaded gun. The culture provides the knowledge or know-how on how to use the knife or the gun. Without this "controlling of the knowledge" the knife or gun may be used against the interest of the user or the owner. Of what use is it that one sharpens a knife or loads a gun only to use either of them against his interest or the interest of his people? Is it not an exhibition of idiocy, stupidity, and in fact insanity?

All right, look into the African societies with its population of academic elite. They must count in millions. Then look at the social ills that new civilization, new money, new culture, new religion, new god–in short, the European style of life–brought into Africa. Even look into the British civil service in Britain or that of the United States. Look at their roads, telephone systems, their attitudes to their work and to themselves, then look at how they present themselves to the world.

I have in actuality seen many Africans with degrees in business and management begging European businessmen to use them as middlemen to exploit their countries. It is the same education, knowledge, and the same schools used to impart the knowledge to the European, American, and African. As a matter of fact, the African in some cases did as well as the Europeans, Americans or better. Then why, for heaven sake why, are the Africans unable to use the knowledge?

The answer is, as I explained above, with the example of the sharp knife and the loaded gun. The African scholars have been able to acquire the sharp knife and the loaded gun, but have lost or did not have the knowledge on how to use them for their own good. They have to work for the European who directs their creativity to be productive.

Look at the African scholar again. He is distasteful. Look at him hiding behind the large desks with the large swivel chairs, making himself a god in an office where he is supposed to be a servant of the people. He is loath-some. Look at him frowning his face at a job he is paid for, pretending to be angry in expectation for bribe. Look at him again sitting at the back seat of the car with his underpaid driver pulling through the gallops caused by the "gaping wounds" on the roads he had the knowledge and power to make smooth. He is repulsive. No, he could not make the road smooth; he has the knowledge and funds all right, but not the cultural power. Look at him drive his own car; he is childishly driving the car like a child playing with a toy. Look at him again, an old man proving that he is civilized by dancing the newest dance step. He is pathetic. Look at him again, a drunken mess, stink-ing in alcohol and cigarette odors–all in his ambition to portray that he is modernized.

It is sad to look at the African scholar. It is shamefully tearful to have the knowledge that this African scholar is an idol the youth are laboring to imitate.

Which Way Africa?

African scholars are thieves. They steal because everybody does it. They steal because what they steal belongs to the nation, and no one cares. They steal because they are protected by the laws and their godfathers. They steal because they are in the position to look after what they steal.

It is unfortunate that Africa has such sons and daughters as the captains of her nations' ships; hence, when they had the opportunity to steer their ships as free nations they piloted them into the worst civil wars in the history of mankind, as in Nigeria, Sudan, Ethiopia, Somalia, Zimbabwe, Monrovia, Angola, Uganda, Egypt, and Algeria. They are still the captains of African ships. Heaven knows what awaits Africa, as these captains are mindless and do not care for what happens to the ships as countries or the passengers as Africans. These African scholars are the idiots that jubilate while their homes are on fire.

So Africans rejoice while their homes are on fire, tooting their car horns on the roads like children with their toys, partying at clubs with loose women from broken homes. It is a gruesome mess these African elite and colonialists have created in Africa. It is not possible that such a gruesome affair is duplicable in the history of man. Both the youths and adults, boys and girls, even infants foam at the mouth, eyes turned murderously red, breathing triple their speed when they are angry. I have seen a taxi driver, who drove at top speed into a group of people fighting, stop the car in the middle of the group at the heart of the road, jump out of the car leaving the engine on while all the passengers in the car rushed out from the taxi only to join the fight with whatever they can grasp.

Africans resort to such secret and deadly methods (when they fail to win the physical fight) as poison, witchcraft, ambush, and blackmail. There was no day mysterious deaths–deaths which could have been avoided with mere common sense and cannot be called suicide or cannot be explained–did not take place in African homes. The sadness goes on and on for the victims understood what happened and vowed to revenge, which they usually succeed to inflict back on themselves.

Such Africans are not distant strangers. They are so close they are their family members. I mean brothers and sisters, parents and their children, cousins, uncles, aunts, such relations.

There is a story of a woman who had a daughter from a man she divorced before marrying another man. The daughter was small when she married the second husband. This daughter grew up to adulthood in the stepfather's home, and decided with the stepfather to get married and conspired to drive out the girl's mother from the stepfather's home, which was her home for she was still married to the man.

The poor mother-wife sorrowfully left her husband to her daughter. This story is complicated and messy, as African society is.

I have also witnessed a father and daughters who conspired and locked up the girls' mother in the police station (cell), because the girls' mother objected to the idea of her husband prostituting their daughters to his friends and strangers. The new Africa is a strange land of strange people and strange happenings. It is a land where the fathers shoot their sons, and the sons machete the parents over money, or where either side should sell the other to parties in ritual sacrifices.

Africa, a continent of conventional mindless inhabitants. They have no feelings for another beings. They do not look back in using the slightest opportunity they have to use, even the life of another human being, to gratify their desires. There have been stories of using even their children to make "medicines" for money, politicians and civil servants using human beings–their fellow Africans–for sacrifices to win favors, elections, and promotions.

The sad thing here is these Africans are the leaders of their countries and see nothing wrong in such mindlessness. They, of course, criticize such things in their countries. They are loud in the criticisms, until they get the power to control affairs in the countries, then some mysterious hands cover their mouths.

Seduction of the Academic Elite

The academic elite is a victim of corruption in their respective countries. The problem of the elite not using their knowledge to rebuild their nations is a different case. It is a case of not being creative.

Any African who is able to pass his school certificate examination is an academic elite, and there are millions with bachelors, masters, and doctorate degrees and different diplomas. These Africans have been exposed to both African social history that is mainly political and economic histories. I know because I, too, am one of the countries' academic elite, for I have some degrees and diplomas as well.

These academic elite are aware that conventional Africa is more than in the continent where the nations stand shoulder to shoulder with other nations of the world, for the nations-Africans are only the instruments of identity for the Africans as human beings in this world. The African is aware of this either from his travels to nations outside his country or from his textbooks.

But the Africa he sees on his return from his travels or after opening the textbook is in many ways different from the picture he has in his mind of what the world thinks of his country or what he thinks his country should be. There are many things he could not believe his country should allow to exist, such things in the nations' capital cities and major cities in the countries: the roads, the inhumane lines at the post offices, banks, hospitals, etc., admission to schools, mindless public servants, poor utility services.

They have seen or read about the Western people and seen how simple it is for them to handle their nations' problems and make the nations a comfortable and happy abode for their people. It puzzles them why Africans' social elite are unable to do such for Africans.

But the African social elite are unable to provide the same social amenities for their people because of corruptions. Africans are corrupt down to the marrow of their bones. Then the young African who has just graduated from his school comes up with theories and determinations to clean his nation, straighten up things, and help his people attain a comfortable and happy life like other peoples of the world. His dear countrymen see such attempts as betrayal and sabotage of their ambitions to exploit their fellow Africans and their nations. Living simple lives according to one's means is a sign of betrayal and sabotage of the corruption system. All Africans want from the academic elite is the "meal ticket"–the certificate which is the passport to position of importance on the nations' economic and political positions.

The Race That Kills Her Sons

The corruption I am discussing in this book is that which induces a public officer by means of improper considerations, such as bribery, to commit a violation of his duty; a departure from the provided standard by the government against the interests of the public; a situation in which a public officer goes contrary to established principles so as to derive certain advantaged either for himself, his cultural groups, or fraternities. Such is a cankerworm that eats and destroys the foundation of any society; Africa, unfortunately, presents herself as a meal to this cankerworm.

Africans, surprisingly, are aware of what they are doing to themselves. They propound ethical standards, emphasize moral scruples, and profess they should be observed. It is annoying, distasteful, and horrible that Africans have shamelessly lost their conscience, for as they preach the gospel or morality they are shamelessly living in immortality and advocating it. They are not even aware of what they are losing or, in fact, have lost.

There are, of course, very few Africans who can distinguish between right and wrong, but these Africans are continuously fighting losing battles to present their points or survive within the environment. There is no consolation anyway that there are a very few Africans who have what may be called conscience because these Africans stand the risk of conversion to a way of life which they loathe. These Africans have no alternative. They are fighting against forces that are greater than themselves. These cankerworms in African society have special ways of appearing to Africans and their disappearing into the veins of African society. From them they dismiss the task carelessly and enliven their hearts with great hopes that all will be well at last.

Such hopes are nothing but mere expectations. Africans sit back with complacency and wait for the gods to intervene, knowing fully well that they (the gods) have not done so throughout their history.

I wonder why the gods have given the conventional Africans such a quality in overdose of ambition for acquisitions of wealth. Their interest for money and wealth is limitless, so limitless that it has no ethical standard. They do not care for what they do or who they hurt to acquire the money or wealth.

How did Africans find themselves in such a mess? Or have Africans recognized that they are in such a mess? Any African who sees such immorality and corruption as a "mess" may not be seen as an immediate danger to Africans. There must be attempts to woo him into the mainstream of the corruption system. Africans do not expect a resistance from such wooing. It is un-African to resist such beckoning into corruption. A resistance invites, immediately, an espionage around the African with the alien mentality to stand up against corruption. Such an attitude invites a dragnet of agents of corruption to either discredit the African or eliminate him out of society.

The African then finds himself in such mental torture that he, too, begins to doubt his moral standard. The resistance is such that the African either joins them, or he drops out of the line, or he is eliminated from the system.

This is the irony in African social life–the system. The system has two arms: one is the social system, which cannot survive without the other, the economic system. This African economic system does not encourage labor, and it is not creative. Productivity is therefore nil in the system. Yet conventional Africans expect the system to sustain them as millionaires. And the system does sustain them.

These systems produce societies which are conclusively abhorrent, that shamefully stand for the symbol of humanity for Africa. This symbol leaves Africa without form and reduced all it stands for as a race of people to be void. It is therefore easy to see the cloud of darkness which hangs heavily over the future survival of Africa's race of people.

The evidence that this horrible disaster is only waiting for time to descend on Africans is not merely prohibited; it can easily be seen among Africans in the street corners, among African drivers, both taxi and private drivers, in African homes among husbands and wives, parents and their children, family relations of various kinds, among friends and professionals, and in fact, is rampant among public servants–in both private and public sectors.

The African physical structures, the nation's functional organs and their products such as schools, religious organs, etc., breed and bleed out such products that are well-groomed to destroy themselves in the system and the organic matters that are responsible for their creation or production. The darkness which hangs over Africa is piteously the kind that has developed profound hatred for the alma mater of such society.

The societies are so stingingly rotten no human being in them can step carefully enough to avoid the stain from corruption. Even the society has recruited honesty as a member of the dragnet in this ugly espionage into corruption. Africans and their nations' physical structures have been designed as agents commissioned to reduce the honest into corruption. There is no being careful in Africa; corruption is a way of life. It is the only way of life in the nations. It is life and living in the society. To stay away from corruption is to stay away from living and watch oneself die slowly. Life means living. Living is not static. It involves motion and participation. Living cannot be done in a vacuum or in isolation. Honesty in Africa must step on somebody or even kick at something. All these must produce some feedback through the system to the honesty. This feedback does not take a mild step for its enemy, honesty is now exposing; it must not only be checked, it must be destroyed and be removed from the corruption den with all possible forces, including the mysterious application of the underground thugs and witchcraft.

Yet Africans live and reproduce to perpetuate this system. One sadly watches this hopeless living and reproducing it with utter disillusionment and despair. Conventional Africans have no hope to offer their children. They even use them to maintain the system by prostituting their innocent carefree children into the ugly and destructive world of corruption. The children, unaware of the dangers of their plights to please their parents, are gradually initiated into the system. I wish Africans could stand outside of their system and see how their future has been ruined and how repair seems impossible.

It is funny that Africans see the wreak of poverty in their cities, villages, and homes, the defiant celebrations of their social elite of their temporary and, in honesty, sudden wealth, their smelling streets with rotten gutters and potholes, mentally deranged Africans hanging around their street corners, their armed robber agents as prostitutes hanging by their hotels and street corners as a mere way of life, and pretentiously or ignorantly refuse to see them as the instruments of self-destruction.

A relation of mine, who shamelessly poses herself as a high class prostitute and her pimp agent who also is a Nigerian academician, told me I am taking these things too seriously. "Nigerians are, of course, mindful of such things, and do not see them as bad as that." I swallowed hard at the nonchalance and cursed the humanity that made the female a relation of mine. She eventually, in her pursuit for negative social identity, reduced me to a beggar in the street before I was aware of her devilish plights. I remember her pimp agent once telling me that whether I like it or not, Africans will still go on with what I call the "underdeveloped conveniences."

I shivered at this and left him, pretending I did not hear him. Yet I have the strong feeling he and my female relation were nervous at my presence, which was actively monitoring their conscience, for not long after he arranged with my female relation to move away from my residence.

This, my relation and her friend, like other Africans, look at Africa as if the corruption and depravity are not enough reason for them to hide their heads in shame. They, at every turn in their lives, tempted the very gods they are assaulting. They have no knowledge of the high level degree of ridicule to which they reduce their creations when, in their heart of hearts, they pay homage to evils and their agents and give only lip service to their gods and race.

How Africa can ever come out from this hopeless mess is only half the problem. The other half lies in the unholy tactics which Africans employ to thwart their chosen path in the country. It is only a matter of time until the Africans harvest the evil seeds they sowed. The harvest is easy. It is based on what is good, and since these Africans have not sown goodness they will not harvest goodness. This logic is simple and clear. If there is any of them who survive the divine process of elimination by death and reach this great day of harvest, as I know many will, the gods will reward them with their wraths.

It is embarrassingly confusing why these Africans have chosen this path of corruption and have lost their senses for survival and preservation of their species, which is the first law of nature. What is it that pushes them as if they are under the spell of the spirits above their control? Why in the name of goodness do these Africans choose the path of destruction, the only road which leads to hell? This is suicidal. Why this desire for self-destruction? How is it these Africans nominate themselves for these appointments to hell?

Africans have never realized they are the architects of their destiny and therefore are the molders of their future and even the present. They are the employers and employees, masters and slaves of Africans. Experience must have taught them this.

A small attempt to understand these Africans poses the question to the curious student: One, who in actuality created these conventional Africans; and why in the name of creation did he create them? If the gods stand for goodness, honesty, truth, virtue, etc., then these Africans should not have been created by the gods or any of them, for these Africans are, in reality, evil. A friend of mine, a true son of the land, who was making a death wish as I had made to stay in this part of the world to straighten the collapsing walls, looked at me knowing full well I was in the ordeal of the herculean task of straightening up the nations' walls and piteously watched these conventional Africans spitting at and stoning me so I would let the walls collapse. He saw me stubbornly dodge the missiles and heard the obscenities showered at me. He, too, was in reality one of them, but with a different view. But when he saw my courage and determination to hold on, he resigned himself the good gods realized I was perishing in my lonely path to restore goodness in the continent and joined me. I shared the hardship with him, and when we began sweating hard in our self-appointed task, he loathfully uttered, "Echezonam, I had wondered why you do all these things. It is not clear to me why we have to do what we are doing. But it appears that we are fighting a losing battle for a part of me, and a good part of me for that matter is telling me that Africans are a race that kills her sons."

Tears formed in my eyes as I heard him draw such a conclusion. I hid my face to save my masculinity.

Yes, Africans are a race that kills her sons. Africans march into the battle fields only to be rich. But the soldier is tamed in the battlefields; he does not shoot those on his side. He is schooled to kill only his enemies—unlike these Africans. They are not tamed. They do not only kill those on their side and their enemies to be rich; they use the dead bodies for missiles or extract all they could from them, including the tooth fillings of the dead. What type of god created these Africans? It is a question that continuously eludes the curious mind.

Africans know full well how murderous their societies are, marching into the battlefields with a single-minded hope to be rich. Parents push their innocent children to the battlefields. Make it or die there. They tell their children, friends, and relations to ostracize those who, out of cowardice or true perception of the evils, attempt to back out. Of course, ostracism does not work any more in Africa. It is only a temporal measure. You either join the system or get weeded out.

But none are weeded out, because Africans volunteer themselves for the system. The system attracts them, for they are surrounded with poverty and none likes the environment. They feel ashamed of themselves, their homes, and culture, up to the standard of despising their languages. Those who can afford ran out from their villages, towns, countries, and even from the continent.

But Africans, unfortunately, cannot afford to be any other thing than what nature made them to be. Conventional Africans do not reason this way. They can fake their existence and connive with unfortunate ones whose plights to be rich had not paid as the assumed lucky ones. Yes, the lucky ones—the adventure to be rich has not paid off to any African. The so-called rich ones are rich only through propaganda, covered up with a car, a house, a wife, a bevy of loose high school dropouts or local female teachers or nurses, a packet of cigarettes, bottles of beer, and a loud mouth telling his mates his adventure into the African money battlefields. This is a wealthy African, and those who have not made it are passing sleepless nights scheming on how to "make it."

They usually choose to leave their residence. They flee from their homes to discover a taste of freedom in the money jungle, where a smile may mean a bait to dupe the next person, prostitution may mean such money to get a four-walled house with an iron sheet cover or even a car, or joining the underground or a fraternity may be a quick solution to the quick money.

Leaving home must start with the unexpected luxuries, normally with sex, cigarettes, and alcohol. Then comes the means to maintain such luxuries with regular employment or employment that may not be able to bear the weight of such luxuries.

Then there follows less sex, less pleasure, and a quick dive into poverty worse than what he left at home. But this is temporary, for the system is there to be maintained, and some people have been sent to recruit them to carry out only a few orders, and all will be well. They can now roam the streets, hotels, and public and private services, and all will be well and even better. The money flows through inflated contracts, prostitution, counterfeiting of different kinds, trafficking in human merchandise, etc.

The African is no longer self-pitying, pursued with sleepless nights or restlessness. No more hunger pangs, he can now tell his friends he plans to write his memoirs. Disco, the loved music which blasts through deep-sounding speakers is the megaphone which says it all, that the African has "arrived" in the money home. He has taken to short cut, avoiding the long road for the economic arrival.

Follow the sound from the disco, and you will surely "butter your bread" that day. Hang around the disco, and you must feed fat from the crumbs of food which miss the rich man's mouth. The disco and the car are the baits, because as one hangs around for the bread crumbs of the riches, he is drafted into the sect of the occult of the rich.

They see themselves in their daydreams on how they, too, will "arrive" with their cars and disco.

How prepared are these recruits? Their definitions answer the question. They are high school dropouts, and those class six youths who could not get into secondary schools. They include university graduates who rely on eye-services to the administrative bosses in their places of employment.

We must not forget this book is discussing espionage into corruption—the problem of leadership in Africa. African leaders are expected to be these immature, lip and eye-service Africans. A young man who was campaigning for promotion in an educational establishment where I was involved as an administrator and had petitioned to the governing board of the establishment against the administrative boss on maladministration and financial mismanagement, told me he knew my boss was all that bad, but he was not the one to tell him that because if he told him, the administrative boss would stop his promotion. Sure enough, this young lecturer has risen from lecturer II to lecturer I, to senior lecturer, and now to principal lecturer in one and a half years. He comes to work at 9:00 A.M. to 9:30 A.M. and goes home at 1:30 P.M. every day and takes off whenever he likes.

It is important that I mention the above paragraph to assure the reader I have not forgotten the theme of this book. Returning to my review of corruption in Africa, the system discourages the honest and rewards corruption agents. Nigerians describe this in the pidgin-talk: "Monkey de work baboon the chop."

The discouragement is so much that where the honest personnel persists on his way, he could be pushed out from the upstairs to the base of unemployment, where he will despise himself and may die of shame. He cannot get up by changing employment. He has been blacklisted. To make a fresh start is to confess his sins to the corruption dragnets, who in turn convey the confession upstairs to the corruptions agents—the boss. It is only then his job is given back to him, even with promotion.

Such Africans are those who sell their souls for a mess of porridge. And that is what Africans are. The African has arrived in the corruption den. He is converted. There he will stay. It was to this dark den of corruption in this alien Garden of Eden in the heart of Sodom and Gomorrah that Fate has been leading him since the date of his birth. He is there, he is held, he is home. The dirty world of corruption, the heartless espionage of corruption has drafted him to determine the fate of Africa. Leadership is there knocking at his door. It has been there waiting for him for a long time, waiting in patience, timeless nights for the inexorable arrival for the corrupt agent. His assignment has been planned, shaped, and reshaped, worked out, and experimented on against the wills of the nature and destiny of man. But for all those years of honesty, through the bloody, futile conclusion of history, the assignment was being made ready for his welcoming into the occult of iniquity. The African is now welcomed into the den. He is not going to be there for a few hours, not for days or for months or years. He has been welcomed to the den which works against his very survival for life. And this is the fate of Africa—a race that kills her sons.

The conversion of honesty into corruption raises some questions. Honesty is described in these simplest terms without ambiguity to mean without deceit or fraud; upright; sincere. If honesty is what it is supposed to be, can it be compromised? Can honesty be converted into corruption as we are seeing in this review of an aspect of African social life? The answer is obvious. Honesty is made of sterner stuff. It cannot be compromised. So the Africans who claim they are honest and sell out to corruption were not honest to start with.

The conversion, meanwhile, has to be tested. There had to be many nights of fear carrying out the assignments on corruption. Corruption in Africa, like all forms of living, is seen by its agents as a game of life. Even the tragedies are regarded as the casualties in the game, until they become personalized. Then the agent starts seeking consolation and revenge by forming or joining another counter-corruption occult still at the expense of the race.

The African seeking revenge is the same African who is now wielding power to combat his corruption boss. Things have changed. Make no mistake about it, corruption may be bad; it has not only given him riches, it has in actuality made or restored his manhood. It has given him power—power to amass wealth and to defend it. And as these two corrupt elephants fight in the African hall to defend or guard their personal interests with African income and property, African walls crumble and the future of the race is obliterated. This is the story of leadership in Africa.

Africans are aware, fully aware, of the shattering effects of their corruptive ventures. It is sad their actions do not jolt their feelings with the formless cataclysm. They are not shaken by the emotional backwash of the fantasy of their action. They are not drowned or even soaked in guilt of their actions. Africans see all these misdirections of efforts and national economy while they live in misery, doing nothing. If when, naturally, an African awakes to the fact that such should not be allowed to go on, it is because he claims he has conscience. Through this, he tries vainly to restore sanity within his people.

What happens here is such an African has stirred the corruption nest, alerting the dragnets of the corruption espionage of both wings of corruption among the people. To the devilish world, a wild boar has invaded their vineyard; he should be converted or removed. Both forces set themselves immediately to work at him, and we can imagine the fate of the concerned African with conscience.

What I write here sounds like fiction. Yet it is not fiction. Look around you—you find them in shapes or moral laxity, nepotism, bribery, fraud, all under the umbrella of secret societies. They do not seem remotely real until the impact of their reality, then one begins to feel their presence. The African can then recall fully well all the trivial actions which led to his sudden awareness.

These trivialities he now recollects have thrown people into disarray. Confusion has reigned. The constituted authority is just there. The nation stays there with disintegration, no authority, and no plans. No social amenities for the people; only these who belong to the corrupt occults have even the double shares of the amenities. What does one do in a situation like this—resign or join them? Africans have answered the question with their notorious saying: "If you can't beat them, join them." And those who refuse to join them get it. They are weeded out until they make it into the six-foot of earth or become made in the streets.

These "rebels" who refuse to indoctrinate themselves in the system go to their graves or become mentally deranged. So they say their actions are heroic. Those who now brand the actions of "rebels" heroic, where were they when the heroes were taking risks to save the race? What glory was there in death or insanity? The problem of fighting corruption must be born by all and not a few who may have the foresight of the threat of corruption among the people. The forecast that reveals the meek will be trodden upon while corruption agents inherit the earth. They are these bloody butchers of innocent and helpless who run down the people to satisfy their selfish ends; while the meek and the idealistic pursue moral values, corruption agents murder them with reality, the reality of self-preservation.

Yes, this is civilization, and it has turned into a festering sore of guilty fear, shameful avarice, mass hypnosis, sanctioned slaughter of the innocent who dares to say what they see, and general blind hatred teaches them by pointed fingers. The world of aesthetic dreamer has died in Africa. The age of faceless system had arrived leaving all the opportunities to corruption syndicate.

Africa has become the continent which teaches her sons not to get frightened, sentimental, or brave when the time comes to the money battlefields of black marketeering, promotions, arm robbery, prostitution, and all the vices designed to strangle Africa. They learn panic leads to fear which proves further panic. Sentimentality leads to foolish bravery, and bravery leads to the grave, and there is no one maxim—the only one there is, is survival. And if that calls for cruelty, if that calls for cunning—that is what you must be. Africa now warns her people this is the era of sanctioned suicide, of blessed mass murder through the result of mass negligence or even mass executions. Africa now pulls at the ears of her sons, you must remember all these when you get out of your doors in the morning.

Corruption has stamped its own kind of brand on Africa. African nations are like dogs, hunched tensely with teeth bared waiting for the assault. There are no outward changes to be seen in the countries—the people still flow through the nations, streets, school children and market women move up and down. In fact, life still goes on yet the change is there—a new degree of tension is present. Africans now live their daily existence against a hidden undercurrent of fear; eyes strained more than usual toward the brooding atmosphere while ears listen to the distant throbbing which would herald the attacks of the correction daredevils to be brothers. Brothers have ceased to be brothers, children have ceased to trust their parents, friendship has turned to a thing of the past.

Still, nightclubs and motels are springing up in African cities as never before. Businessmen, politicians, and civil servants form the nucleus of a nocturnal existence which was basically a roar of conversations—alcohol, cigarettes, sex, and black marketeering. Men and women now shamelessly cling together in the shaded lighting of the clubs with sweaty, emaciated desire, thighs trembling against willing partners. The dance unfolds a prelude to seduction. Cheap liquor, cheap entertainers, and cheap prostitutes—all of them commanding high prices in the new order of the corrupt world. Africa has turned to this.

Africans live now in this dirty world of sins and sex. They live in the world of illicit money, gained from the black-market, moving from club to club, night after night, with drink after drink, surveying the wild, blind, desperate faces around them and generally criticizing the world they carved for themselves. These are the people we call Africans and their leaders—the social elite.

Situations in Africa have given birth to the human vultures we call our leaders, who take advantage of the weak and those with a degree of ethical consciousness and grow fat in the nations' predicament. Leadership should be qualified with the concern for the people who are being led.

African leadership has no concern for the enslaving African mass. A relation of mine, by marriage, who was a top official in one of the states' ministries and who also calls himself a concerned Christian, told me once the enslaved mass in Nigeria is destined to servitude fate. Africans have destroyed the love of a child for his mother. Even the love for what is decent is no more in Africa. Money has taken their places. It is the love for the almighty money that matters to Africans. Seek ye first the African wealth and all other things will follow.

Here Africa is reborn in the biblical Sodom and Gomorrah with its corruption dens in the underworld of easy money, loose sex, drunkenness, and endless intrigue of an underworld society, built on sin and evils, where blackmail and coercion walk hand in hand with the assured hope that corruption has always triumphed in African societies. The gods and their mortality can always be worshipped with the blood of the innocent and the honest ones who look down on corruption. The self-appointed social elite, in their new morality of stepping on the downtrodden Africans to acquire money, now survey their kingdom, moving back and forth furtively and fiercely through the blue smoke and loud music and golden glasses of beer to count the blessings Mother Africa has showered on them.

These African leaders have said goodbye to the eras of gentle heart and opened their doors to welcome the incoming generation with their American ghetto talk. This is the Africa and her people waiting for a return to the era of Murtala Muhammed or the era of the Ghanaian Rawlings. Such men do not come every day, and when they come, they do not live long, for Africans will attempt to corrupt them, and when they fail, bump them off as they took care of the great General Muhammed in the street. Yes, that is Africa all right. They will perpetuate themselves on the blood of the honest Africans who dare question the ethics of their actions. Africans under such leadership are too blind to see where they are going. So they blunder on and fearfully follow the orders of the day—corruption from one state of confusion to another state of confusion, taking no note of their mistakes and making no corrections while the corrupt world feeds fat on the nations' troubled world.

Africans are so corrupted that they turn evils around them and discount the taxes on their own immoral actions. They have sold out the human dignity, surrendered the pride and pain of choice, and passed over the moral burden of their own actions onto their fraternities.

This is an act of moral cowardice. It works for them, but it destroys the nation. As long as it works for them, they try to perpetuate the system, but for how long will the nation bear the burden of the masses at the pleasure of the few who believe that the honest and innocent masses will continue to tolerate to be downtrodden forever? The masses can rebel. History has recorded such before in other human societies. Africa's case will only be an addition to the records. Rebellion is not the solution, for the masses still suffer the punishment from such social disorder while these corrupt social elite still fish and feed fat in the nations' troubled waters.

Africans believe they can find the contentment in life by denying its reality. The fact is Africa has changed and the change is for the worse. The brutal outcome of corruption is now affecting African masses. Africa is surely coming to its meaningless end. Africans live, obviously, in deep despair. And the despair is worse than pain, because pain is transitional. Pain can move beyond feeling. One can crawl through pain and come out again. Africa's social ills are problems which are not transitional.